49th Fighter Group

Group

Aces of the Pacific

Aviation Elite Units • 14

49th Fighter Group

Aces of the Pacific

William N Hess

Series editor Tony Holmes

Front Cover
Heavily involved in the Southwest Pacific campaign in New Guinea and New Britain, the 49th FG was in the vanguard of Allied air operations in one of the toughest combat theatres of World War 2. For much of 1943, its units covered bombing raids on the Japanese stronghold of New Britain, off the northeastern New Guinea coast. One such mission took place on 28 July, and the official entry for this date in the 49th FG's war diary read as follows;

'The 9th Squadron again scored in an interception on 28 July. Nine P-38s were escorting B-25s to New Britain. Twelve to fifteen enemy aircraft, believed to be "Oscars", were observed three miles off the north coast of New Britain, midway between Tamuniai Island and Cape Raoult. Capt Jim Watkins took the score of the day, adding three to the four he had carded on the 26th. Lt Dick Bong downed one "Oscar" definite, Maj Sidney S Woods one "Oscar" definite and one probable and Capt William F Haney and Lt Ralph H Wandrey one "Oscar" each, both probables.

'Capt Watkins submitted the following combat report;

'"I took off from Horanda Field at 0639 hrs, leading 'Captive Blue Flight'. I proceeded on an escort mission to Rein Bay, New Britain. We covered B-25s as they proceeded around the coast towards Cape Gloucester.

'"We were at 6000 ft when we sighted 12 to 18 enemy fighters 3000 ft above us off Cape Raoult at 0815 hrs. We dropped belly tanks and the flight turned 90 degrees into the attack. I fired at the attacking leader and missed. I climbed to 8000 ft out to sea and made a head-on attack at one of two 'Oscars' attacking Lt Bong. This aeroplane burst into flames about 75 to 100 yards in front of me.

'"I turned to find Lt Bong and made a head-on attack on one of the three 'Oscars' coming down on me. This ship burst into flames, and pieces of this ship barely missed me as he passed under. The other two didn't bother me.

'"I went back towards the flight in a steep dive. At 4000 ft I levelled out to meet a head-on attack of two 'Oscars'. Neither one would meet me. The lead ship of the attackers

pulled straight up into a stall at about 6000 ft. I fired a long two- or three-second burst into him while he was hanging on his prop, and he went straight into the sea, exploding as he hit. I got in several more short bursts at the others but was then chased off."'

Capt Watkins was flying P-38G-10 42-12882 on 28 July 1943, and the trio of Ki-43s credited to him during the course of the mission gave him ace status. He would down three more 'Oscars' in this aircraft just five days later (*Cover artwork by Mark Postlethwaite*)

First published in Great Britain in 2004 by Osprey Publishing
1st Floor, Elms Court, Chapel Way, Botley, Oxford, OX2 9LP

ISBN 1 84176 785 9

Edited by Tony Holmes and Bruce Hales-Dutton
Page design by Mark Holt
Cover Artwork by Mark Postlethwaite
Aircraft Profiles by Chris Davey
Index by Alan Thatcher
Printed in China through Bookbuilders

04 05 06 07 08   10 9 8 7 6 5 4 3 2 1

EDITOR'S NOTE
To make this series as authoritative as possible, the Editor would be interested in hearing from any individual who may have relevant photographs, documentation or first-hand experiences relating to the world's elite units, their pilots and their aircraft, of the various theatres of war. Any material used will be credited to its original source. Please write to Tony Holmes via e-mail at: tony.holmes@osprey-jets.freeserve.co.uk

ACKNOWLEDGEMENTS
The author would like to thank Steve Ferguson and John Stanaway for their generous help in providing additional photographs for inclusion in this volume.

For details of all Osprey Publishing titles please contact us at:

Osprey Direct UK, P.O. Box 140, Wellingborough, Northants NN8 2FA, UK
E-mail: info@ospreydirect.co.uk

Osprey Direct USA c/o MBI Publishing, P.O. Box 1, 729 Prospect Ave, Osceola, WI 54020, USA
E-mail: info@ospreydirectusa.com

Or visit our website: www.ospreypublishing.com

CONTENTS

FORGING THE 49th

When Nazi Germany invaded Poland on 1 September 1939, the United States Army Air Corps (USAAC) had 26,000 personnel and fewer than 2000 aircraft. The start of the war in Europe prompted its steady growth, but the fall of France the following summer made national defence a priority virtually overnight. The Army Air Corps was handed what amounted to a blank cheque, and in July 1940 the Department of War created the Army Air Forces as its aviation element, and soon afterwards raised its status to equal that of the Army ground forces.

One of the new formations which sprang up was the 49th Pursuit Group (PG), which came into being at Selfridge Field, Michigan, on 20 November 1940. It comprised the 7th, 8th and 9th Pursuit Squadrons with 130 non-commissioned personnel and nine pilots under the command of Maj Glen Davasher. Ill-health, however, forced the latter to relinquish his post, and he was succeeded by Maj John Egan in February 1941.

Group establishment remained static until May, when the 49th PG was ordered to a new base at Morrison Field in West Palm Beach, Florida, with 19 officers and 280 enlisted men. By then it had yet another new CO in the form of Maj George 'Snuffy' McCoy. His squadron COs at this time were Lt Allen Bennett (the 7th), Lt Robert Van Auken (8th) and Capt Victor Pixey (9th). A 75-truck convoy conveyed most of the unit's equipment south from Michigan to its new home in Florida. Training of

Ex-49th FG COs Col Bob Morrissey and Gen Paul Wurtsmith (then head of V Fighter Command), converse at Tadki in April 1944. Later that year Morrissey was severely injured (he lost a leg) during the invasion of the Philippines when his ship was bombed (*Steve Ferguson*)

Brig Gen Paul 'Squeeze' Wurtsmith was head of V Fighter Command from late 1942 until relieved by Brig Gen Freddie Smith in March 1945. Wurtsmith was a career aviator who had enlisted in the Army in 1928 and earned his wings four years later. Given command of the P-40C-equipped 49th PG just five days after the attack on Pearl Harbor, he led the group into action in the defence of Australia in early 1942. Despite being promoted 'upstairs' to Fifth Air Force HQ, Wurtsmith would periodically sneak off in his personal P-38 in order to perform combat sorties with the '49ers'. Such flying earned him the unswerving devotion of his pilots. Awarded a second star, and promoted to major general, Wurtsmith was made commander of the Thirteenth Air Force on 1 March 1945. He was subsequently killed in a peacetime flying accident (*Steve Ferguson*)

both pilots and ground personnel progressed through the summer, but this was very limited due to a paucity of modern equipment. Indeed, the squadron's flying strength was confined to single examples of the Stearman PT-17 and Ryan PT-13 trainers, three obsolete Seversky P-35 pursuit machines and one Curtis P-40 fighter per unit. Training was inevitably leisurely, and curtailed even further by persistent mechanical problems with the elderly P-35s.

Matters changed, however, on 7 December 1941 with the surprise Japanese attack on the US Navy's Pacific Fleet in Pearl Harbor. There were multiple changes in its wake, with Maj Paul Wurtsmith assuming command of the 49th PG, while the 7th PS was taken over by Lt Robert Morrissey and the 9th PS by Lt Jim Selman – Van Auken remained in command of the 8th PS. Training intensified, and flight hours doubled during December.

OVERSEAS

On 4 January 1942 the 49th embarked on a four-day train journey to San Francisco, where the men were herded into the County Livestock Pavilion to be joined by thousands of others en route to the Pacific. Once the unit had recruited 75 new pilots and over 500 enlisted men, it became the first USAAC fighter group to be posted overseas following America's entry into the war. On 12 January, the bulk of the 49th PG embarked on the USAT *Mariposa*, with the remainder sailing aboard the SS *Coolidge*. On 1 February both vessels arrived in Melbourne, Australia.

It was the first stage of a journey that would take the group to the thick of the fighting in New Guinea and the Philippines. By 1945 it was on the verge of a move to Okinawa for the final assault on the Japanese Home

The US Army's first ace of World War 2, Boyd D 'Buzz' Wagner claimed five 'Nate' fighters in four days while leading the 17th PS during the ill-fated defence of the Philippines in December 1941. Wounded in action, he escaped to Australia in early January 1942 and was temporarily seconded to the recently arrived 49th PG by V Fighter Command the following month. Here, Wagner gave the unit's novice pilots the benefit of his combat experience. Promoted to lieutenant colonel, Wagner returned to the Pacific in April 1942 when he led P-39s into action for the first time over New Guinea. Claiming a further three victories in his first action with the Bell fighter, Wagner was eventually posted home in the autumn of 1942. This photograph was taken soon after his return to the USA (note the P-47B Thunderbolt in the background). Having survived the fall of the Philippines and the early battles of the New Guinea campaign, Wagner was killed in a flying accident (at the controls of P-40K 42-10271) near Eglin Field, Florida, on 29 November 1942 (*Author*)

Islands when the atomic bombs were dropped on Hiroshima and Nagasaki. In the process, the 49th would also transform itself from being a 'green' unit to a battle-hardened fighter group, with a formidable reputation as the top-scoring outfit in the Fifth Air Force. Its list of aces included Dick Bong, who became the USAAF's top scorer.

All that lay in the future when, on arrival in Australia, the 49th's three squadrons were sent to different fields for combat training. The 7th went to Bankstown, in Sydney, the 8th to a Royal Australian Air Force (RAAF) airfield east of Canberra and the 9th to Williamtown, near Newcastle, north of Sydney.

The 49th's P-40Es had been shipped out with the group (19 aboard the *Mariposa*, 32 on the *Coolidge* and seven as deck cargo aboard the SS

Monroe), and they had to be assembled and flown to the various bases as quickly as possible, for the men had been told that they would have just two weeks to get ready for combat – a tall order for pilots with so little training on their aircraft. Wurtsmith immediately requested assistance, and was fortunate to get Capt Boyd 'Buzz' Wagner, the first Army Air Corps ace from the Philippines, to help establish the training syllabus. Each unit received 25 P-40s, and each aircraft was thoroughly tested. The biggest problem facing the pilots was learning to combat engine torque on take-off, and many ground loops occurred. Indeed, some 30 accidents were recorded in the first two weeks.

INTO ACTION

On 4 March Maj Wurtsmith asked 7th PS CO Lt Morrissey if he had enough combat-qualified pilots to send a detachment to Horn Island – a remote airstrip hundreds of miles away in the far northeast at the tip of Cape York, in Queensland, and only 75 miles south of Japanese-held New Guinea. The pilots had to use maritime maps for navigation, and of the 12 P-40s despatched, only nine arrived at Horn Island. To make matters worse, the flight had been arranged so quickly that no transport had been organised for accompanying groundcrew. Pilots would therefore have to do their own servicing, or depend on what help they could find at the two-mile wide spit of land that was Horn Island, in the Coral Sea.

The Japanese had landed at Lae, on the northeastern coast of New Guinea, and were confident they could capture Port Moresby. On 14 March they sent eight Mitsubishi G4M bombers (given the Allied code name 'Betty' in the autumn of 1942), escorted by a dozen A6M2 Zero fighters, to find out if the hasty bolstering of Allied defences in northern Australia would affect their offensive. At 1230 hrs Morrissey was warned about the approaching hostile formation and he immediately scrambled his nine aircraft, which formed up at 10,000 ft and began to orbit over Horn Island. The 7th PS CO ordered his pilots to test their guns, but discovered that only one of his functioned. He immediately returned to the airstrip in order to clear the jams, before rejoining his formation. Later, Morrissey reported what happened next;

'We had been flying around for about five minutes when I saw eight Japanese bombers at 12,000 ft, 15 miles out to sea and flying back in the direction of New Guinea. To the rear of the tight formation of bombers, a lone fighter, which I presumed to be Japanese, was flying back and forth off the tails of the big aeroplanes. Keeping in mind that fighters accompanied the bombers, I jockeyed our formation to attack the eight aeroplanes. While I was looking around to size up the situation, and just before I attacked, nine Zero fighters came into view also at approximately 12,000 ft, but some 7000 ft below us. I turned to attack the fighters.

'At that time I had but three two-ship elements in the formation. The Japanese fighters were flying a close "V" made up of four three-ship "Vs". I decided to attack the leading Japanese element and let my second and third elements attack the consecutive Japanese ones. I proceeded to attack with my wingman, Lt A T House. My second element hesitated momentarily because the attack signal was not received clearly, and as I passed the second Japanese element they began shooting at me. Lt House saw what was happening and shot one Zero down, but at this point his

Four men who served with the 49th from the group's early days in Australia until they became senior commanders are pictured in Darwin in 1942. They are, from left to right, Paul Wurtsmith, Bob Porter, George Prentice, who became the 475th FGs first CO in May 1943, and Don Hutchinson, who led the 49th FG from November 1942 (*Steve Ferguson*)

guns jammed so he flew directly across the top of another Zero fighter and deliberately dipped his wing into the Jap's cockpit. The Japanese fighter crashed, but Lt House, despite the loss of approximately three feet of his right wing, made a safe landing.

'I shot one Zero in the first element, but dove out without attacking another because I saw bullets being fired at me from behind. I didn't see the fighter which I shot go down, but knew he had taken enough of my 0.50-cal bullets to destroy him. Lt House later verified this with the statement that he saw the ship dismantle in mid-air immediately after my pass at him.'

Lt Clarence Johnson was also credited with downing one of the Zeros. Lt Harold Martin went after the bombers alone and fired at all of them before he singled one out and pumped his remaining ammunition into it. A naval report later revealed that a twin-engined bomber had crashed into the sea near where the combat had taken place. The 49th PG had scored for the first time, but not without loss, for Lt Sanford had been forced to ditch his aircraft at sea. With the 7th PS detachment soon reduced to just two aircraft within a matter of days, it was ordered to abandon its post.

At around this time the other units of the 49th PG commenced another long journey which would mark the beginning of the campaign to defend the northern Australian city of Darwin. As the Japanese continued their drive towards Port Moresby, they began to concentrate their attacks on Australia by pounding Darwin, which was still receiving refugees from Java. New enemy units moved into airfields in Timor, and on 3 March Zero fighters destroyed aircraft and attacked port installations. This attack caused great concern in Australia, and resulted in the call for the 49th PG to be moved to the Darwin area as soon as possible. First to depart was an advance party from the 9th PS, which was immediately followed by the air and then ground detachments.

Capt James Selman set out on 8 March on the 2000-mile trip to Darwin with 25 P-40s. Numerous storms and maintenance problems delayed them, and it was not until the end of the month that the 21

This publicity shot of Lts Bruce Morehead (right) and Andy Reynolds was taken at an RAAF base near Darwin in May 1942. The P-40E behind them was assigned to the 7th FS's Capt Bill Hennon, who, just three months prior to this photograph being taken, had emerged from the disastrous defence of Java as the sole American ace. The fighter featured a red spinner, which many Philippines and Java veterans in the 49th FG painted on their aircraft, stars around the nose, a flight leader's band around the rear fuselage and a large 'Bunyap' screaming demon design, which the 7th FS later adopted, on the rudder. This P-40 was eventually wrecked in a collision. Hennon went on to score seven victories before completing his tour, and he later disappeared on a cross-country flight in March 1943 after returning to the US (*Steve Ferguson*)

surviving aircraft arrived at their destination. But they were soon on the move again, as the unit's assigned RAAF base was found to be too badly damaged by recent enemy raids to allow it to support further flight operations. The 9th PS duly took up residence at Batchelor Field, some 50 miles south of Darwin.

The unit's novice pilots were now joined by some experienced men who had seen combat in the ill-fated defence of the Philippines and Java. Capts 'Buzz' Wagner and Walter D Coss were assigned to Headquarters

Taken on the same day as the photo above, this shot shows Lt Andy Reynolds posing astride the cockpit of future ace Lt Bob Vaught's P-40E *"BOB'S ROBIN"* (*Steve Ferguson*)

Java veteran Capt 'Bitchin' Ben' S Irvin, who was 9th FS CO for a short period in Darwin, leans against the wing of his P-40E (41-25164, 'White 75') *The Rebel*, showing its prominent Pegasus fuselage art. Irvin had claimed two confirmed victories with the 17th PS in February 1942 before joining the 49th PG. Irvin did not add to his tally while leading the 9th FS, and returned to the US in late October 1942 (*John Stanaway*)

Squadron, while Lts Nathaniel Blanton, Jack H Dale, William J Hennon and Lester J Johnson went to the 7th PS and Lts R B Dockstader, George E Kiser and James B Morehead joined the 8th PS. Finally, the 9th PS was boosted by the arrival of Lts Joseph J Kruzel, Ben S Irvin and Andrew J Reynolds. Those assigned to the 9th were immediately sent to Darwin, while the others went temporarily to Bankstown.

FIRST BLOOD

It was to be the 9th PS which drew first blood over Darwin when, on 22 March, Lts Clyde L Harvey Jr and Stephen Poleschuk encountered a Mitsubishi Ki-15 'Babs' reconnaissance aircraft. Poleschuk related;

'We were on patrol at 1000 hrs at 20,000 ft. We sighted one "Nakajima 97". I don't think our approach was observed. I delivered a 30-degree beam attack, closing to less than 200 ft in a slight climbing turn, firing 100 rounds. The enemy made a 180-degree diving turn and then a shallow climbing turn to the right, probably to look back. The enemy aeroplane was shot down in flames. The pilot baled out.'

Lt Harvey also made a diving attack, but apparently did not fire.

The squadron was back in action on the 28th when a flight of four Warhawks, led by Lt Mitchell Zawisza, intercepted seven G4M bombers. Harvey sighted the aircraft at 19,000 ft and followed them seven miles out to sea. He dived down on one and flew through the rear gunner's fire in order to get up under the bomber's belly, where he delivered a burst and the G4M caught fire. Lt Robert Vaught reported;

'I was the last aeroplane to attack the formation. The attack was made from the right beam and above. After the first pass, I made another from the left and drifted directly behind the left side of the formation of six. A stream of black smoke came out and the plane went into a spin and crashed into the ocean. That left only five ships in the formation – the right engine of the next ship from the left was burning. He was losing altitude and dropping from formation. I don't believe it made it back to base.'

The attackers were credited with downing three of the seven bombers, with Lts Vaught, Harvey and William Sells the victors. There were two more encounters before the end of the month, but only Lt Andrew Reynolds was successful, accounting for a Zero in a dogfight on 31 March.

BIG SHOW

The 9th PS enjoyed more success on 4 April, when two flights of P-40s (14 aircraft) intercepted seven G4M bombers, escorted by six Zeros. All the G4Ms and two of the fighters were destroyed, but two P-40s were lost and Lt John D Livingstone was killed when he attempted a crash-landing following the combat. Lt Grover Gardner was downed over the sea by a Zero, but he baled out and was rescued. Lt Andrew Reynolds related;

'We were on patrol near Darwin and I was leader of the formation. We were at 26,000 ft over Darwin, and were in a V-formation. The attack began over Darwin Bay and continued over Cox Peninsula. We sighted the enemy over Darwin, seven miles south of the township. There were five bombers in extended V-formation and three Zeros in V-formation 20 ft above and behind them as escort. We delivered a diving head-on attack. The Zeros were completely surprised, and attempted to climb. I downed one Zero and one bomber. A second bomber was shot down by Kelting. Our losses were nothing in this combat. Two of the aeroplanes mentioned fell in flames and one pilot was observed parachuting from his aircraft.'

Lt John Landers had engine trouble all the way to the combat area, and when he did catch up, he sighted only two straggling bombers. He dived on one and sent it smoking down into the undercast. The second bomber was already badly damaged. Landers gave it the *coup de grace* and the aircraft fell in flames. Finally, Lt John Sauber was credited with a bomber and a Zero in the combat.

The 7th and 8th PSs arrived in the Darwin area in April, the former moving to Batchelor Field, the latter to Adelaide Field and the 9th taking up residence at Livingstone (originally 34-mile strip, this base had been renamed after the 49th PG's first combat fatality, Lt John Livingstone).

On 25 April – ANZAC Day – 50 P-40s from all three squadrons intercepted 24 bombers, escorted by nine Zeros, in the the largest Japanese raid on Darwin in months. The top-scoring squadron was the 8th PS, whose pilots claimed ten bombers and a Zero shot down. Lt James B Morehead accounted for three 'Type 97' (actually G4M) bombers, while Lts Richard Dennis and Edward Miller each got a pair. Morehead reported:

'I took off and climbed to 19,000 ft and sighted about 24 twin-engined bombers, escorted by a number of Zeros. The bombers were headed out towards the sea, and my

Lt 'Big John' Landers served with the 9th FS during the defence of Darwin. After scoring six victories in the Pacific, he went on to greater fame as a group commander in the Eighth Air Force, flying P-51s. His final score was 14.5 aerial victories and 20 aircraft destroyed on the ground (*Steve Ferguson*)

flight happened to have the altitude on the accompanying flight, so I dived (bombers being at 14,000 ft) and intercepted the enemy at the tip of Melville Island. I throttled back completely on my approach and fired a long burst at the leader of the flight, dropping him from the flight. I did a steep turn and came up just under the right echelon of ships. Fired on two bombers in this echelon dropping on to the tail of the rearmost aircraft, so I did a steep turn to the right and came in on his tail and sent him headlong into the sea.

'Another bomber was straggling back at this time, so I pulled in on his tail and he went into the sea too. I looked back and a Zero was on my tail so I dove and pulled up steeply, sighting another Zero which I met head-on and probably damaged, but did not get for certain, as he pulled away sharply at about 8000 ft. As I turned to attack this damaged Zero, I found I had another on my tail, so I dived away and pulled up steeply and found about five Zeros at a great distance out to sea. I climbed, but my engine was smoking slightly and throwing oil on the windshield, so headed for home port.'

Morehead's great day was spoiled when his landing gear failed, although he was uninjured in the subsequent crash.

HEAVY LOSSES

Following this heavy defeat, the Japanese were eager to get their own back on the 49th. This was achieved on 27 April when 17 Japanese bombers attacked Darwin, escorted by nine fighters. In a heated battle, the Americans downed three bombers and four Zeros, but paid dearly when four P-40s fell to the opposing fighters. Two pilots were killed. Lt Earl R Kingsley of the 8th PS reported;

8th FS pilot Lt Alford plays the organ during the Sunday Service at the 49th FG's makeshift chapel at 27-Mile strip. Chaplain Roby is giving the service to the right of the organ (*Steve Ferguson*)

Long-suffering groundcrewmen pose for the camera while changing the engine of an 8th FS P-40E at Strauss Field in mid 1942. Note the total absence of maintenance stands and specialist servicing equipment (*Steve Ferguson*)

'Capt Strauss (squadron CO) led his flight – myself and Lt Alford – to the right of the enemy just before they dropped their bombs, and misjudged their speed and distance to the extent that we went in just behind the bomber formation. When Lt Kingsley saw that Capt Strauss had misjudged the leading formation, and was turning in behind the bombers, and that the Zeros on his tail were also in a position to fire, we both turned into them hoping to at least scare them off. Capt Strauss saw the Zero, pumped the stick a couple of times, then turned right into a very tight turn. The Zeros started firing.

'I, having missed the bombers, also turned to assist Capt Strauss, and a second Zero cut in front of me, apparently trying to cut off Capt Strauss from the front. I shot him in the belly and he went down. The first Zero was then shooting, and tracers were just missing Capt Strauss' tail. A Zero, according to Lt Alford, came down from behind and high to the left and was firing on my tail from directly behind. I dove to 17,000 ft and chandelled to the left, as the bombers turned to the left. I climbed parallel to their course and on the left side of them until, well above them, I made one pass at a Zero and three bursts at the bombers. Two were hit in the middle of the fuselage without apparent damage. There were six Zeros with the bombers and I left them.'

Capt Allison Strauss apparently fell to the guns of the Zero on his tail and crashed to his death near the port of Darwin. Like Lt Livingstone, Strauss also had an airstrip south of Darwin named after him soon after his death.

During the same action, Lt C C Johnson, with Lt Otis Fish as his wingman, made a head-on pass at a Zero, but found himself under attack from behind. He was able to break and dive away, but Fish apparently took fatal hits from a Zero and his P-40 crashed into the water. Lt Harvey Martin of the 8th PS was also badly shot up by a Zero and forced to crash-land near Cape Charles.

On a more positive note, following a head-on pass through the enemy formation, Lt George Kiser was credited with shooting down two of the bombers and a Zero. The 7th PS's Lt Stephen W Andrew also engaged a Zero head-on, shooting it down, but his P-40 was badly damaged in the process and he was forced to take to his parachute. Coming down in the water, he managed to swim to shore.

COMBAT IDENTITIES

In the wake of this sharp action there was a lull as Japanese aircraft were reassigned to support ground forces advancing across New Guinea. A few bombers remained at Koepang, in Timor, but their night missions were little more than a nuisance. This break enabled the men of the 49th Fighter (Pursuit was dropped by the USAAF in May 1942) Group to become more settled and organised in their quarters. At the same time they were able to assume their combat identities.

The 9th FS at Livingstone Field, under Capt Selman, adopted the insignia of a winged knight's helmet on a blue shield, with a red band running diagonally from the upper right to the lower left behind the helmet. The 8th, based at the newly renamed Strauss Field, became identified with its leader Capt Ed Sims, and its pilots were seen as a liberal and mischievous bunch who lived up to their nickname, the 'eight balls'. Meanwhile, at Batchelor Field, home of the 7th FS, there was friction between some of the unit's senior officers. When it was settled the unit adopted the insignia of the screaming demon, which had been displayed on the aircraft of veteran ace Bill Hennon. It depicted a mythological Javanese jungle demon called Bunyap, which was said to possess great powers. So it was that the squadron became the 'Screamin' Demons'.

The lull was ended abruptly on 13 June when Japanese aircraft returned to Java after the Port Moresby campaign. Maj Van Auken, 49th FG Executive Officer, and Lt Ben Brown were on a training exercise when they were alerted that enemy aircraft were reported heading for Darwin. Flying at just 5000 ft, the two P-40 pilots spotted the attacking force heading towards them at very high altitude. Van Auken finally positioned himself behind the bombers, but his wingman had to drop away at 17,000 ft because his aircraft could not keep up. After a long climb, Van Auken finally reached the bombers' altitude. Afterwards, he reported;

'Made an attack from the left rear after evading two Zeros which attempted to head me off. Fired a burst into one bomber and dove away, coming up about three miles on the other side of the formation. When attempting to get into position for another attack, I was surprised by an attack by Zeros, who put 20 mm "slugs" in my wing. I dived and pulled out at 10,000 ft. Could not pull out with the stick, so was forced to use the stabiliser.

'At this point I was again attacked and received more hits. I believe this was the same pair of Zeros that first attacked. I went into another dive and pulled out at 300 ft. I looked back and saw that the enemy was still on my tail. They shot at me again and my aeroplane caught fire. I opened the canopy and unfastened

Capt Ed Sims took over the 8th PS following Capt Allison Strauss' death in action on 27 April 1942. A laid back character, Sims set the tone for the unit, which soon became known as the 'Eightball' Squadron. He had downed a G4M bomber on 25 April 1942 while flying this machine, which was marked with his own personal insignia (*Steve Ferguson*)

This P-40E, flown by the 8th FS's Lt Monty Eisenberg, ground looped and turned over at Strauss Field on 13 June 1942 after returning from a major engagement over Darwin. Eisenberg emerged from the wreckage with only minor injuries (*Steve Ferguson*)

my belt, preparing to bail out. I pulled up to 800 ft and slow rolled, intending to drop out at the top. When a quarter of the way around, with my wings vertical, the ship seemed to be hit with a torrent of bullets and went out of control completely, starting to drop. This threw me back into the cockpit. I put my arms and head into the slipstream which pulled me out of the aeroplane. I immediately pulled the ripcord. One of the Zeros fired a burst at me while I was descending in the parachute. This was the last attack.'

Van Auken landed in shallow water 150 ft from shore.

The 8th FS also had a patrol up at this time, and once alerted, the P-40 pilots headed after the bombers. Lt Pierre Alford was still climbing to reach the enemy bombers, which were at 23,000 ft, when he was jumped by a Zero – he later stated that he had not seen his opponent. Alford attempted to dive away, but the Zero stayed with him until he bailed out at around 2000 ft. As he descended, he saw two Zeros manoeuvring to shoot at him. It was at this moment that Lt Earl Kingsley arrived on the scene. Kingsley had sighted two aircraft down low, which were flying wide apart, and were obviously not P-40s. He reported;

'One of them made a 180-degree turn while they both circled wider inland and then turned 90 degrees toward the coast and headed out to sea. It was then that I saw the parachute. Both aeroplanes attempted to strafe the parachute. I dived on them to prevent them strafing again.'

One of the Zeros was shot down by Kingsley. The squadron's suffering was not yet done for the day, for Lt Dick Dennis landed a badly shot-up Warhawk and Lt Monty Eisenberg ground-looped his, inverting it in the middle of the strip. Finally, Lt C C Johnson, who was wounded by 20 mm fire, bellied his P-40 in beside the strip.

JAPANESE RUSE

The 14 June raid was most unusual, as the Japanese sent as many as 25 Zeros over Bathurst Island towards Darwin, while just nine G4M bombers approached the city from a more westerly direction. Their ruse worked, and none of the 26 intercepting Warhawk pilots saw the bombers. A 7th FS patrol, flying at 20,000 ft and led by Capt Nate Blanton, roared in to attack the fighters. Blanton downed one Zero and probably another, but Lt Keith Brown was picked off by two enemy fighters and forced to bail out. He came down near Batchelor field, breaking a leg when his parachute got caught up in a tree. Then it was the turn of a dozen 9th FS P-40s, led by Lt Andrew Reynolds, to engage the enemy. A fierce fight ensued, and after some 30 minutes Reynolds, Jack Donalson and John Landers had each downed a Zero. All 12 P-40s returned safely to base, but some had suffered battle damage.

The following day the size of the raiding bomber force was increased to 27, with some 15 escorting Zeros also in attendance. Their target was fuel storage tanks, but little or no damage was done. The 49th put up 28 P-40s, with the 9th FS scoring against the Zeros. Lts George Manning and Robert McComsey each shot one down, while Clarence Peterson and Thomas Fowler shared a third.

The 7th was also in the thick of the fight, as Hennon and Capt George Prentice both scored. The sixth Zero of the day fell to Lt Claude S Burtnette Jr, who also damaged a bomber. A Zero put a burst into the wing of Burtnette's P-40, shooting off part of the aileron and knocking the cover off the ammunition boxes. He managed to spiral his damaged fighter down to 2000 ft, where he bailed out, being recovered from the water soon afterwards. Lt Clarence Johnson scored hits on two bombers,

Right
Lt James A 'Duckbutt' Watkins shows the nose art on the starboard side of his P-40E's cowling. Watkins claimed just one victory in P-40s (on 26 December 1942 after the 49th had moved to New Guinea), but went on to add ten more kills after the 9th FS converted to the P-38 in early 1943. His last victory came on 2 April 1945 while he was serving a second combat tour in 49th FG headquarters (*Steve Ferguson*)

Below
Lt Watkins flies over Darwin in his first P-40E, 'White 72'. This aircraft is sometimes illustrated with a plain white star on the fuselage, but close examination of this photo reveals it had the standard blue disc behind the star (*John Stanaway*)

but he too was forced to bail out after a Zero set his aircraft on fire. He landed on Cox Peninsula, south-west of Darwin, and was forced to a make a five-day trek home after losing his boots when his parachute opened.

On the 16th the Japanese launched what was to be their last raid on Darwin for the month. Again, a force of 27 bombers, escorted by 15 Zeros, attacked the Darwin area, successfully striking fuel storage tanks. Two of the tanks were hit, and fierce flames burned into the night. Although 36 P-40s were airborne, they destroyed just one bomber and one fighter. And the cost of these successes was high, with the 8th FS losing Lt Chester Namola when his fighter was hit by a Zero and sent spinning into the harbour. His body was never found. Squadronmate Lt Harvey Martin was forced to crash land in shallow water just off the beach at Cox Peninsula.

Lt William Harris was determined to destroy at least one bomber after seeing the two P-40s shot down, but his guns jammed. He then ran out of fuel and was forced to walk home after crash-landing in the Fog Bay area.

More successful was Lt Andrew Reynolds of the 9th FS, who reported;

'I was over Darwin with four ships and got into a position to attack the bombers but we had to go over ack-ack so we went west and intercepted the bombers two minutes after Capt Kruzel's flight had hit them. I was at about 29,000 ft, and the bombers at about 23,000 ft. There were 27 bombers in flights of nine turning to the right. Approximately 18 Zeros were scattered all about. Some were still diving after Capt Kruzel's flight. We made a diving attack from above and almost along the line of the echelon.

'The flights were all lined up. I attacked the highest flight. They were firing a bit from the top gun turrets after I shot bursts into the bombers, but I kept shooting until they went by. Zeros were shooting on the way down. I shot bursts into all nine bombers in the flight I attacked. The first one burst into flames and was going down and the second ship was also on fire and was dropping behind when the Zeros attacked me. A shot, probably from the bombers, damaged my aeroplane in the oil and coolant systems. I landed, wheels up, in a small field.'

Capt Tom Fowler flew P-40s with the 9th FS from Darwin in 1942, and then switched to P-38s when the squadron was re-equipped in early 1943. He shot down a single Zero with the P-40 and two more with the P-38 (*John Stanaway*)

Lt Leon Howk poses alongside Lt John Sauber's P-40 before it was destroyed in a mid-air collision with Lt George Preddy's Warhawk on 12 July 1942. Sauber, who was probably killed when the two aircraft collided, was found in the wreckage of his fighter (*Author*)

Lt George Preddy was badly injured in the mid-air collision on 12 July 1942 which killed fellow 9th FS pilot Lt John Sauber. The future ranking Mustang ace is seen here standing alongside Capt Joseph Kruzel's P-40E-1, marked with a dragon artwork, at Strauss Field. Another 17th PS veteran who had claimed three kills over Java, Kruzel led 'Dragon flight' during the 49th's defence of Darwin – hence the personal marking on his Warhawk (*Steve Ferguson*)

Lt John Sauber of Reynolds' flight maintained his element during the attacks by the Zeros and managed to shoot one of them down. It was to be a short-lived triumph, for on the afternoon of 12 July Sauber suffered a most unfortunate accident.

He and new pilot Lt George Preddy had taken off to practise fighter tactics, Sauber hoping to teach his wingman how to escape an attack. The tyro climbed above his mentor and dived to begin a mock attack, but he misjudged the distance between the two P-40s and flew into Sauber's machine, probably killing the latter pilot instantly. Although injured, Preddy was able to bail out, and after several months of recovery, returned to the US. There, he was assigned to the newly-formed 352nd FG (see *Osprey Aviation Elite Units 8 - 352nd Fighter Group* for further details), which was subsequently posted to England as part of the Eighth Air Force. Preddy subsequently became the war's top-scoring P-51 Mustang ace.

VAUGHT'S PASSENGER

No tale of the 49th FG's early war fighting in northern Australia would ever be complete without a mention of the varied experiences of the 9th

FS's Lt Bob Vaught. On 16 July he had just taken off on a routine patrol flight when he became aware that he was not alone in the cockpit. There, slithering around between his rudder pedals, was a three-foot snake! After a few hurried foot movements, the snake sank its fangs into Vaught's leg and held on. The pilot immediately grabbed the reptile by its head, pressed hard enough to open its mouth and threw the snake out of his open canopy. Vaught was quite alarmed as his leg began to tingle and, unaware of the species of snake, or the potency of its venom, he felt that he should get down as soon as possible.

Vaught immediately landed at a sheep station, but could find no help. By this time his leg was swelling and throbbing, so the pilot climbed back into the cockpit of his fighter, only to be surrounded by water buffalo which bumped against the aircraft. A short burst from the guns scared the animals away, and Vaught then went to sleep. The next morning it was obvious that his leg needed attention, and Vaught managed to take off and get home. He was immediately taken to hospital, and a week's rest seemed to restore him to full health.

A further respite enabled the 49th to take stock of its situation. While the plotting of inbound raids had improved greatly, the group was still finding it difficult to intercept enemy formations at the right time and place. The high altitude of the attacks was unexpected, and the P-40's slow rate of climb put the defenders at a further disadvantage. However, the pilots who had fought in the defence of Java had infused the group with valuable combat experience at just the right time, although they were struggling to ensure that novices employed the correct attack and dive tactics in the heat of battle. The American pilots had also quickly discovered that they were unable to manoeuvre with the nimble Japanese Zero – a factor which had emerged in combat with the bomber escorts during the hectic June raids.

NIGHT RAIDS

The bombers returned between 25 and 29 July. Two flights of three to five aircraft came each night, circled the target areas and dropped an assortment

Its engine removed for routine maintenance, a P-40E sits quietly amongst the trees at Strauss Field in mid 1942. The 49th FG operated with limited facilities, parts and tools in its fight to defend northern Australia from Japanese raiders during 1942 (*Author*)

Lt I B Jack Donalson scored three confirmed victories over Nichols Field, in the Philippines, on the first day of the war, and later escaped to Australia. There, he joined 'Blue Flight' of the 9th PS/49th PG and participated in the defence of Darwin. Donalson is seen here with the second of two P-40Es named *MAUREE* that he flew in 1942. He received this machine as a replacement for P-40E-1 41-24809, which he wrecked in a twilight landing on 16 June. Donalson scored his fifth kill on 30 July flying replacement *MAUREE* P-40E-1 41-36090 (seen here) (*John Stanaway*)

P-40E-1 41-25164 *"Texas Longhorn"* was the second Warhawk assigned to Lt John D Landers in 1942. 'Big John' scored six Warhawk kills during his tour (*John Stanaway*)

of bombs, most of which exploded harmlessly in the bush. There were a a few isolated interceptions, but none was successful.

Daylight raids resumed on the 31st when, at noon, 27 bombers appeared in the customary three V-shaped formation, with an escort of 15 to 20 Zeros. They were met by 27 P-40s of the 49th, which downed six Zeros and three bombers. The 7th FS's Lt Gene Duke was shot down in return. He reported;

'My attack was head-on, trigger pressed until within a very short distance of the enemy bomber. He staggered, wavered, dropped below me and caught fire, as was told to me later by other members of my flight. After he dropped away, I chandelled into the third flight, which was to the left and above me. My bullets seemed to have little effect on the lead ship, so I dropped down to about 2000 ft before starting to climb back up again. It was at this point that my motor began acting up. Fumes rose in the cockpit, and a solid sheet of oil covered the windshield. Finally, I had sense enough to look behind me, and there were two aeroplanes on my tail, which appeared to be firing. I bailed out and landed on the beach. I was picked up by a patrol boat.'

Lt Edward Steere had a different view of the action, and filed the following report when he got back to base;

'I sighted enemy bombers at a height of 3000 ft, with Zeros at 5000 ft, directly west. My approach was apparently unobserved. I dove out of the sun from above to attack the enemy when my target pulled up to avoid my attack. As I was shooting at the enemy, one Zero seemed to explode in the air, but another turned and shot at me and I dived out. They had formed a funnel behind the bombers. I observed one Zero going down in flames at Charles Point, which Lt Posten claimed. There were 15 to 20 Zeros above the bombers and behind, going out, which formed a sort of circle formation, losing and gaining altitude. Their position was to the rear and above the bombers. The main force bombed, turned and then went home.'

The 9th FS tangled with the Zeros 35 miles off the coast on their way home, claiming four destroyed. Lts Jack Donalson, Clay Tice, Andrew Reynolds and John Landers all scored victories.

The enemy now reverted to night missions, which achieved very little.

This change of strategy coincided with significant personnel upheaval

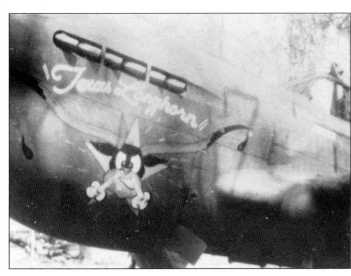

Assigned to the 49th after his escape to Australia following combat with the 17th PS (with whom he claimed 3.5 kills) in the Philippines, Lt John H Posten added a single Zero kill and a probable while flying with the 7th FS in northern Australia in 1942 (*John Stanaway*)

within both the 49th FG and its controlling organisation, the Fifth Air Force. Lt Gen George H Brett was succeeded by Maj Gen George Kenney, who made numerous changes in the headquarters staff and throughout the command. Col Wurtsmith was appointed CO of V Fighter Command, being succeeded as 49th FG CO by Maj Don Hutchinson, who had been standing in for Wurtsmith while he had been at GHQ, Brisbane. Capt Morrissey left the 7th FS to become deputy group CO, while Capt Bill Hennon took over leadership of the 'Screamin' Demons'.

The 49th FG's P-40s made their last interception over Darwin on 23 August 1942. The 27 G4Ms arrived in V-formations, with 15 to 20 Zeros bringing up the rear as usual. But this time instead of coming in over the harbour, the Japanese formation headed for Batchelor and Strauss Fields to the south of Darwin. The defending pilots were greatly assisted in their interception by recent additions to RAAF radar and radio facilities.

As a result, it was now possible to engage the raiders miles before they reached their targets, and 21 P-40s made contact with them. The 8th FS, led by Capt George Kiser, and including Lts Marlin Smith, Donald Morse

Yet another engine change is performed on an 8th FS P-40 at Strauss Field in mid 1942. The ability of the groundcrews to keep so many aircraft flying in such conditions was nothing short of miraculous (*Steve Ferguson*)

and George Davis, attacked the bombers head-on some 25 miles from the coast. Four of the bombers were hit hard, and three dropped out of formation trailing smoke. Kiser, Smith and Morse were each credited with their destruction.

Four 7th FS pilots – Lts Ray Melikian, Wilson Chapman, George Drake and Donald Lee – met the attackers ten miles west of Fog Bay, the bombers flying at 25,000 ft, with Zeros flanking them on either side. The P-40s hit them in a diving attack, which apparently took the Japanese by complete surprise. Drake downed a bomber and a fighter, while Melikian and Chapman each got a Zero. A second flight from the 8th FS intercepted the bombers just before the coast, and Lt Charles Johnson shot down a Zero in flames.

Just after bombs away, Lts Posten and Vodrey from the 7th FS shared a bomber and Lt Lee flamed a Zero. Another 7th FS flight chased the bombers back out to sea as they fled home, and while several were undoubtedly damaged, only Lt Frederick O'Riley was credited with having destroyed one. A flight from the 8th FS also pursued the G4Ms, but failed to locate them, although it did shoot down three of the escorting Zeros. Lt James Morehead accounted for two and Earl Kingsley got the third.

The 49th FG had lost only a single aircraft during the course of this lengthy engagement. Lt O'Riley had continued to pursue the bombers until he ran low on fuel and was then forced to crash land on the beach at Finke Bay.

All in all, it had been a great day for the group, with seven bombers and a record eight Zeros shot down. It was a fitting finale to the group's defence of Darwin.

Lt Donald H Lee (left) of the 7th PS flew _"BITZA-HAWK"_ from Batchelor Field during April 1942. By the time he finished his tour in the summer of 1943, he had four victories to his credit (_Steve Ferguson_)

JUNGLE WARRIORS

The Japanese followed up their conquest of the Dutch East Indies by invading New Guinea in April 1942, and by mid-year they were driving south towards Port Moresby, on the southern coast – uncomfortably close to northern Australia. Plans for an amphibious landing had been frustrated by US resistance at the Battle of Coral Sea in May, forcing the Japanese to take the overland route across the formidable Owen Stanley mountains following landings on the northern coastline of New Guinea.

It was an inhospitable area, with sharp ridges of flesh-tearing stone and the putrefaction of thick jungle through which flowed black mud. The task of preventing the Japanese from reaching their objective was mainly in the hands of Australian infantry, supported from the air by the RAAF and also by the USAAF. By early September the campaign in New Guinea had reached a crucial phase, and the Australian troops were fighting tooth and nail to hold on. They needed help desperately, and the P-40s of the 49th were ordered move to the Port Moresby area as soon as possible.

Lt Randall Keator was credited with two Zeros destroyed while flying with the 20th PS on 8 December 1941 – the day the Pacific War began in the Philippines. He is shown here in Port Moresby in 1942 while flying with the 49th FG. Although standing amongst the wreckage of what appears to be a downed Japanese aircraft, Keator did not claim any further victories with the latter unit (*Author*)

Aircraft of the 7th FS were flown from Darwin to Townsville, in Queensland, on the 7 September for overhaul and repair, with the intention of ferrying them to 14-Mile Strip, near Port Moresby, once they were ready. The 8th FS also flew its P-40s to Townsville, but the unit would not move on to New Guinea until there was room for them. While in Townsville the aircraft would receive belly plumbing and shackles to enable them to carry either 75-gallon fuel tanks or a 500-lb bomb.

FIRST BATTLES

On the 11th the 7th FS set out for New Guinea, which was a long haul for the Warhawks. Three days later Maj Morrissey arrived with a dozen P-40s at 14-Mile Strip, and by the 19th they were bombing targets in the hills. Another flight attacked barges and a fuel dump with good results. The following day the 7th FS joined up with P-400s from the 41st FS to attack Kokoda aerodrome and destroy two bridges.

On the afternoon of the 21st ten P-40s took off for the Kokoda-Buna area on their first dive-bombing assignment. An important bridge was bombed, and the hits achieved were sufficient to make it unusable. Pilots also strafed and destroyed a building, several barges and a motor launch.

In late September Australian troops began their efforts to push the Japanese back down to the Kokoda trail – a jungle track running through the Owen Stanley Range along the eastern side of the mountains. The primary weapon they lacked was heavy artillery, and it was then that Brig Gen Ennis Whitehead of the Fifth Air Force agreed to make Capt Bill Hennon's 7th FS the 'mobile artillery' for the Australian forces on the Kokoda trail. The pilots flew multiple missions every day and became

9th FS veterans of the defence of Darwin prepare to fly to Port Moresby in November 1942. They are, from left to right, Dick Taylor, Stephen Poleschuk, Clay Peterson, John Landers and Fred Hollier (*Steve Ferguson*)

proficient in dropping bombs onto enemy forces that were in close contact with Australian troops and attacking their fortified positions.

It was at around this time that Gen George Kenney also honoured an earlier promise that he had made to the 49th FG during its defence of Darwin. He had told the unit that it would receive P-40Ks as soon as they arrived in-theatre, and in October the first of these was delivered to the 7th FS at 14-Mile Strip. The K-model Warhawk boasted a new supercharged Allison engine that gave more power at lower altitudes, thus enabling it to carry bomb loads of up to 1000 lbs. Its high altitude performance was not improved, however.

In late October it was 8th FS's turn to move. Although now tour-expired, unit CO Capt Ed Sims agreed to lead the squadron to New Guinea, although he was not permitted to fly combat. The 8th had its old E-models overhauled, and these were also supplemented by aircraft

The 8th FS's flight engineering section at Three-Mile Strip, near Port Moresby. Note the jungle immediately behind the supply shack (*Author*)

Lt Ray Melikian's P-40K *Swing It* made a belly landing while being flown by Lt Dillworth in November 1942. The aircraft was subsequently broken up for spare parts (*Steve Ferguson*)

Another view of Lt Melikian's aircraft after its gear-up landing in New Guinea (*Steve Ferguson*)

discarded by the 7th FS, which had now completed its conversion onto the P-40K. The 8th took up station at Three-Mile Strip, which was also the home of the A-20-equipped 3rd Attack Group.

The unit wasted no time in getting into action alongside the A-20s, flying escort for them on 29 October when they attacked Japanese-held airfields at Lae. They repeated the mission on 1 November when the P-40s strafed the runways on one of Lae's primary airfields. Lt Richard Dennis led one section of four Warhawks, and as they dropped down low on their way home from

the target in order to skirt cumulus clouds, they were jumped from above by eight Zeros.

Dennis and his wingman, Lt Bill Day, dived and then pulled up steeply to engage the enemy. while the second section, comprising Lts Ross Baker and Glenn Wohlford, continued downwards. Before they could recover from their dive, Wohlford took hits from two Zeros in the tail section of his P-40 and smoke began to pour from his aircraft. Seconds later it plunged into the jungle. As Dennis pulled up, he was able to hit one of the Zeros with multiple strikes on its engine during a head-on attack. The cowling and then the engine itself broke away and the Japanese fighter spiralled into the ground. Day fired at two more Zeros before he finally

Lt Bill Day of the 8th FS with his P-40E-1 *JERRY* at Three-Mile Strip in December 1942. Day would become an ace on 11 March 1943 when he shot down a Zeke and a 'Betty' during an interception mission over Tufi Point (*Steve Ferguson*)

His fighter (41-35972 *JERRY II*) marked with five red 'meatballs', Lt Bill Day converses with his crew chief Ed Gillam in New Guinea soon after 'making ace' (*Steve Ferguson*)

flamed one. Since the odds were still against the Warhawks, both pilots dived away and headed for home.

NEW EQUIPMENT

On 16 November the 9th FS moved its P-40s to Four-Mile Strip. Here, senior pilots continued to man the aircraft while others waited for the unit's new twin-engined P-38 Lightnings to complete operational modifications and arrive in-theatre. The following day all three 49th FG units escorted C-47s hauling supplies to a new advanced strip.

The 7th FS was involved in another scrap on an escort mission to Lae on 22 November. En route to the target, the Warhawk pilots sighted six bomb-carrying Zeros on their way to attack Allied ground forces. The P-40s went to investigate and duly engaged the enemy, Lt Irving Voorhes making a head-on pass that caused the enemy fighter to burst into flames. The pilot bailed out. Voorhes then latched onto a second Zero, but had to take cover in the clouds when he noted tracers passing over his wing.

Lt Paul Slocum also made a head-on pass at one of the Zeros, but when he saw another on the tail of a P-40 he immediately went to the latter's rescue, sending the enemy fighter down in flames. Slocum then teamed up with Capt William Martin to chase two more Zeros along the coast. Martin finally made his strikes tell on one of them and probably destroyed it. Lt Kenneth Johns also engaged a Zero, and at the same time saw Lt Don Sutliff, who was on the tail of another, take a cannon hit in the wing of his P-40. Sutliff turned for home, but was forced to bail out over swamp land, from which it took him 21 days to return to base. Less fortunate was Lt Don Dittler, who was last seen by Johns with two Zeros on his tail.

There was more action in the Lae area on 26 November. Lts Bruce Harris and Earl Kingsley had led two 8th FS newcomers on a fighter sweep

Lt Deems Taylor was one of the early flight leaders within the 9th FS in 1942. Here, he poses beside the colourful dragon which signified aircraft of 'Dragon Flight' (*author*)

to Lae that morning, and as they circled the airfield Harris decided to take Lts Warren Blakely and John Porteous down to 8000 ft – below heavy cloud – for a closer look. As they broke through over the Markham River, they sighted a formation of Zeros and circled down until the were chasing the enemy fighters over the tree-tops. As things tightened further, they wound up in a Lufbery circle, with the Warhawks and the enemy on each other's tails. Harris finally chased his opponent into a steep canyon, and when the Japanese pilot tried to gain height the P-40 pilot hit him with a burst which set the Zero on fire.

Moments later, the Japanese pilot on Harris' tail tried to disengage but he was so low that Blakely fired at him from point blank range and the Zero literally fell apart. Lt Porteous finally got onto the tail of another Zero, where he was joined by Kingsley. They opened fire at the same time and their victim was last seen heading into the cloud base trailing smoke.

There was another big fight on 30 November, when 16 P-40s from the 7th FS were providing top cover for the 8th, which was in turn dive-bombing Buna. Attacked from above by a dozen Zeros, Lt Donald Lee got on the tail of one of the Japanese fighters and fired at it. The enemy pilot snapped into a stall turn and came back at the P-40 head-on, but a burst from Lee set the fighter ablaze. Lts Irving Voorhes and John Johnston were both shot down, but another Japanese pilot paid the price for passing in front of Lt Frank Nichols when his flight joined the scrap. Firing from point blank range, Nichols sent the Zero down in flames.

Lt Sheldon Brinson attacked two Zeros at once and managed to shoot one down. He then made the near-fatal mistake of watching his victim's demise, and found another Zero on his tail, forcing him to run for cloud cover. Lt Lucius Lacroix caught a smoking Zero heading for home, latched onto its tail and despatched it with a solid burst. Finally, Lt Howard Nelson caught a Zero in a stall and finished it off with a burst into the cockpit.

By now the dozen 8th FS P-40s had completed their dive-bombing mission, and they too became involved in a series of dogfights. Lt Robert Moose joined two other Warhawks chasing a Zero, and when the enemy pilot attempted a vertical reversement, Moose caught him with three bursts. With its wing almost severed, the Zero went down in flames. Lt Harold Learned fired at another Zero head-on and sent it down before its pilot could fire a shot. Another fighter caught Lt Bryant Wesley with cannon and machine gun fire, wounding him and forcing him to roll the P-40 over on its back and bail out. Wesley, who had to swim ashore, struggled through swamp land for two days before finally making it home.

NEW ALLIED BASES

By early December 1942 Japanese attempts to seize the Kokoda trail had been thwarted by the Australians, who now joined up with other Allied forces in the offensive to drive the enemy north along the coast of New Guinea towards Buna. If the latter fell, territory would become available for new bases from which the Allies could strike Lae and even the Japanese bastion of Rabaul. Fifth Air Force had not only been highly successful in its ground support missions against enemy troops and installations, but had also managed to secure local air superiority. Now, Allied airmen were determined to prevent Japanese reinforcements reaching Buna.

Capt Frank Nichols' 7th FS P-40 is serviced by one of the few fuel trucks in New Guinea. Note the American Volunteer Group-inspired markings on the fighter's nose. Nichols was credited with four victories flying the P-40 in 1942-43, before helping establish the 475th FG's 431st FS in mid-1943 and 'making ace' flying the P-38 (*Steve Ferguson*)

On the first anniversary of the Pearl Harbor raid, Capt Frank Nichols of the 7th FS was leading a flight of four P-40s in the Buna area when he received word from the ground station that a large formation of enemy bombers was inbound from Lae. A few minutes later the Americans saw some 18 Mitsubishi G3M Type 96 bombers escorted by a dozen Zeros. Nichols positioned his flight above the enemy and led them in a head-on attack. Clouds had apparently hidden the approaching P-40s, allowing Nichols to attack one of the bombers as soon as he was in range. He scored numerous hits on the right engine and wing of his target.

At that moment, the Warhawk pilots half-rolled and dived to prevent interception by the Zeros, and as the flight pulled out, two large fires were seen on the water below. The second bomber had been downed by Lt John Hood, who riddled the right engine of his target and then poured another very long burst into the cockpit area. Both the stricken bombers had dropped out of formation before the attackers had dived away in order to make good their escape.

Minutes later the 9th FS's Lt Robert Vaught led his flight into position above the bombers, before initiating his attack. Diving through the formation, he pulled up beneath the bombers and fired long bursts into two of them. Both 'Nells' dropped out of formation and went down in flames. Lt Duncan Meyers came in behind him, firing into a third bomber, and although a Zero attempted to engage him, he sent it down in flames. Lt William Levitan shot down a fourth bomber and was then thrown into a spin that slammed him around in his cockpit so violently that he broke his goggles. Six bombers shot down for no loss added up to an outstanding victory for the 49th FG.

FACING A NEW ENEMY

By December 1942 the Imperial Japanese Naval Air Force had suffered great losses in the campaigns against Darwin, Port Moresby, Buna and the Solomon Islands, forcing the Japanese Army Air Force to move into the theatre. The latter would be primarily based at Lae and at Rabaul. As a result, Fifth Air Force would now be facing the vaunted 11th *Sentai*, which had been victorious in China, Burma and Sumatra. The unit was equipped

Capt George Manning's 7th FS P-40 *SCATTERBRAIN* has its magazines replenished and windscreen wiped clean at Four-Mile Strip in December 1942. The aircraft reportedly boasted a bright red spinner (*Steve Ferguson*)

with the nimble Nakajima Ki-43, which would become known to the Allies in the autumn of 1942 by its reporting code name of 'Oscar'. This was just one of more than 100 names devised by the Air Technical Intelligence Unit of the Allied Air Forces to resolve the confusion surrounding the names of Japanese aircraft. From now on fighters would be given male first names and bombers would be known by female first names.

The first big clash between the 49th FG and the 'Oscars' came on 26 December when the 9th FS caught a gaggle in the Dobodura area. Lt James Watkins was leading one of the flights, and he later reported;

'At 1110 hrs we sighted two Zekes (actually "Oscars") at 8500 ft south, southwest of Dobodura. We dropped our belly tanks and dived to attack in two-aeroplane elements. The initial attack was delivered at about 1112 hrs from about 2000 to 2500 ft. Instead of two Zekes, there were about ten. Lt John Bagdasarian chased one off my tail as I was firing at the leader of the lower flight of Zekes. Lt William Levitan closed in to protect me and fired at another Zeke tailing me. Lt Arthur Wenige followed through on the initial attack but failed to score. Lt Levitan and I both observed the first Zeke, into which I fired three long bursts, pull up, begin smoking, and fall off in a spin and crash into the ground.

'I then turned to the left and began firing at another Zero. There were two or three everywhere you turned. This one made a tight turn to the left and I followed, firing at him. He rolled over on his back and I did too. He seemed to stop and then start an inverted spin, with some sort of spray or white smoke trailing him. My guns ceased firing when I was on my back – I didn't realise I was on my back until I tried to get out of the fight. I called my flight and told them not to dogfight with the Zekes. I turned out of the cloud into a dogfight with still more Zekes. One skidded in front of me and I missed him by a good 200 ft. I zoomed right through the melee, in which you could not tell P-40 from Zeke unless you were right on them, and flew back into the clouds.'

Watkins was credited with the destruction of an 'Oscar', with a second probably destroyed, although the latter was never confirmed.

Lt Wenige had a series of scrapes in the same action, including almost flying into an 'Oscar' as he shot out of cloud while trying to flee the area.

A meeting of minds in New Guinea between, from left to right, the 9th FS's Lt Peterson, Capt Sid Woods, Capt Clay Tice and Lt John Landers. Note the fresh-faced Lt Dick Bong in the second row, extreme right (*Steve Ferguson*)

He attacked the 'Oscar' head-on from close range and sent it down in flames. Lt Bill Sells from Watkins' flight scored a direct hit on the fuel tank of another Ki-43 and had the satisfaction of seeing it explode. Levitan chased down another 'Oscar' and sent it down in flames, while Lts 'Big John' Landers and Robert McDaris engaged a flight of enemy fighters in the same area. McDaris was successful in his first pass, destroying one aircraft, but he then lost sight of Landers and decided to head for home rather than going it alone.

Landers had opened fire on his first opponent from a distance of 200 ft, and the 'Oscar' quickly blew up. He then became involved with a second fighter, and after a series of tight turns he managed to send it down in flames. Landers' aircraft had taken several hits during this engagement, however, and heading for home over the mountains, his engine began to fail and he was forced to bail out. The American spent several days in a native village before returning home.

The 9th FS had gained an impressive victory over its new enemy, downing seven Ki-43s for the loss of Landers' P-40E.

The next day the Japanese launched a rare mixed aircraft strike against Dobodura when Navy Zekes and D3A 'Val' dive-bombers sortied with Army 'Oscars'. As the dive-bombers began their attack, the enemy formations were intercepted by two flights of newly arrived P-38Fs from the 39th FS/35th FG. Flying on the wing of flight leader Capt Tom Lynch was Lt Richard Bong, who was on temporary assignment from the 9th FS due to his Lightning experience in the USA. Lynch immediately lined up on one of the Zekes, which disintegrated under his fire. Bong would

Newly promoted 1Lt Dick Bong gives his best steely-eyed stare for the camera at Dobodura in this 6 March 1943 shot. Sat in a war-weary P-38F-5, Bong had claimed his sixth kill just three days prior to this photograph being taken (*Author*)

also be credited with a Zeke, which he had originally claimed as a probable, as well as a 'Val'. In the second P-38 flight was Lt Carl Planck, who was yet another 9th FS pilot on temporary assignment to the 39th FS. He too would be credited with downing a Zeke in this, his first combat.

An incident during this combat was to have repercussions later at debriefing. As the P-38s attacked the enemy, 7th and 9th FS P-40s also joined in, but Lts William Hanning and Birge Neuman were jumped by P-38s which shot holes in both of their Warhawks. Back at Port Moresby, tempers flared, and it was all that Maj Bob Morrissey could do to prevent physical violence erupting. This represented a sour end to a year's combat during which Lt Col Don Hutchinson's 49th FG had scored 100 victories at a small loss in terms of aircraft and pilots.

THE LAE OFFENSIVE

January 1943 saw the Japanese determined to preserve their hold on the strategically important town of Lae, but their embattled troops were in bad shape and in urgent need of reinforcement. So it was that on 7 January the 49th FG attacked a troop convoy en route to Lae. The 7th FS took off first, its fighters laden with 300-lb bombs. The Warhawk pilots had hoped that they would find the ships in harbour by the time they attacked, thus presenting them with static targets, but the vessels were still at sea, and heavily escorted by fighters, which disrupted the attack.

Finally, Lt Frank Nichols was able to drop his bomb on the stern of a ship, probably causing serious damage. Then Lts A T House and Claude Burtnette hit another transport and sank it.

Free of their bombs, the P-40 pilots began strafing attacks, causing multiple casualties among the troops crowding the ships. Then the 8th FS arrived and had a field day, achieving a record 13 aerial victories. Lt Ernest Harris was the top scorer with three. Later, he reported;

'We took off from Kila Aerodrome in a flight of 15 aeroplanes to strafe transports at Lae. I was leading four. Before reaching the target we were attacked by Zeros. My flight split up and engaged the enemy, but I continued on and strafed one transport. I observed pieces flying from the deck of the ship, but was unable to observe other damage. I pulled up into the fight and attacked a Zero that was on the tail of a P-40. I closed in on him, shooting, and saw him burst into flames.

'I pulled up and made a pass at a second Zero. I put three long bursts into him and observed the bullets striking the aeroplane and pieces disintegrating from it. The aeroplane rolled over out of control and into a layer of clouds. I immediately pulled up and made a pass at a third Zero. I pressed the attack to a very close range and fired two bursts into him and saw my bullets striking him around the cockpit.

'The Zero began spiralling down, seemingly out of control, into the clouds. I dove, circling the clouds and getting under them. I observed the aeroplane burning on the water, and two other large circular wakes where other machines had hit the water. These were all in the vicinity of where the Zeros I had attacked had spiralled down through the clouds. The engagement took place over Markham Bay and lasted about 35 minutes. I saw two ships burning besides three transports, one cruiser and at least one destroyer.'

Also in action on 7 January with the 39th FS was Dick Bong, his unit tangling with 'Oscars' which had just taken off from the airfield at Lae. In the ensuing dogfight, Bong was able to down one of the Japanese fighters for his fourth victory. He saw further combat the next day when the 39th was escorting bombers over Markham Bay. Bong met an 'Oscar' head-on and destroyed it to become the 49th FG's first P-38 ace, albeit serving with another group at the time.

On 30 January Col Don Hutchinson was transferred to V Fighter Command Headquarters as Chief of Staff, and his place as 49th FG CO was taken by newly promoted Lt Col Bob Morrissey.

Nicknamed *Betty Boop,* this L-4 Grasshopper was issued to the 8th FS at Dobodura in 1943 for use as a general hack. It played a crucial part in retrieving a number of downed pilots from the jungle during the spring of that year, and remained with the unit well into 1944 (*Steve Ferguson*)

In late 1942 Australian Army engineers had established a new base at Wau, complete with a 4000-ft airstrip, between the mountains. This provided a facility that could be used by American C-47 transports bringing in supplies for the Allied forces on the ground. On the morning of 6 February Capt Frank Nichols led a flight of 7th FS P-40s that were tasked with escorting a formation of C-47s heading for Wau. However, this was also the day when the Japanese decided to send Kawasaki Ki-48 'Lily' bombers, escorted by 'Oscar' fighters, to strike Wau. Nichols described what happened;

'We arrived at Wau at 1045 hrs and had almost made one complete circle around the drome at 15,000 ft when, out of the west, three aeroplanes dove down by my flight. At first I thought they were our bombers, but I then saw the red Japanese discs and, at the same time, looked below and saw three more bombers and lots of Zeros ("Oscars") at 12,000 ft. I dove for the three bombers, which had enough of start on us to be able to drop their bombs before they came within range. As they pulled up from their dive, I was close enough to start shooting, and the bomber's rear gunner also started shooting. I fired a short burst at the bomber and saw my tracers going into it, but as I pulled up over the aircraft it was still flying straight and level. I then turned around to the right and started back to Wau, gaining altitude.

'I immediately attacked a Zero ("Oscar") from the side but missed him, and then another came down from above, firing at me. I had to dive to get away. I pulled back up to 11,000 ft, and to my right I saw a Zero ("Oscar") dive on a P-39. I quickly caught the Zero ("Oscar") from its blind side, as the pilot was busy firing at the P-39. The Zero ("Oscar") began smoking and it started down in a gentle dive, which became rapid. I watched it go all the way down and crash into the mountain to the north of Wau.

P-40K-1 42-46292 *Patsy Ruth* was assigned to Lt Arland Stanton of the 7th FS at Port Moresby's 14-Mile Strip during early 1943. Stanton was a replacement pilot who joined the 49th FG in the autumn of 1942 in New Guinea, where he was assigned to Nick Nichols' 'Nip Nippers' flight. He scored his first victory on 30 November 1942 over Buna while flying with Nichols. In his second combat, flown in this aircraft on 6 February 1943, Stanton shot down a Zero and damaged a Ki-48 'Lily' bomber during a big scrap near the forward airstrip at Wau. Exactly one year later, on 6 February 1944, the young Pennsylvanian scored his fifth confirmed kill (*Steve Ferguson*)

'About this time another Zero ("Oscar") dove on me again from above and I had to dive out. I climbed up again and started shooting at a Zero ("Oscar") which was head-on, but this time his partner, over on my right, half-rolled down and started shooting at me. Again, I turned into that one and dove out. I climbed up, and this time saw another Zero ("Oscar") coming at me head-on, so I held my fire until I was within range and started firing. He pulled up and exposed his belly right in my face. I fired a long burst into him and then he burst into flames and went into a spin. This time his partner meant to get me, and started down on me. I dove down, and the Zero ("Oscar") followed me down quite a way, but finally gave up the chase. After this I climbed back up and couldn't see any more aircraft.'

The C-47s had a grandstand view, however, and left the area. In total, the P-40 pilots accounted for seven of the enemy. Lt David Allen got two of the bombers, and single fighters fell to Lts Don Sutliff, Robert Greene and Arland Stanton.

The same day 9th FS P-38Gs were in action for the very first time, four of the Lightnings joining up with aircraft from the 35th FG on a mission to Lae. En route, they encountered 'Oscars' over Wau, and Lt David Harbor caught up with one in a dive and hit it hard enough to send the fighter down in flames. This was the first P-38 victory for a pilot flying under 9th FS colours, the unit having swapped its Warhawks for Lightnings during January 1943.

Further significant changes in the 49th FG command structure took place at the end of February when Capt Sid Woods became 9th FS CO and veteran Maj Ed Sims was finally relieved by Capt Jim Porter as boss of the 8th FS.

BATTLE OF BISMARCK SEA

Having failed to repulse the US invasion of Guadalcanal in September 1942, and then surrendered Buna to Allied forces by year-end, the Japanese were determined not to lose Lae. Their first convoy of reinforcements had been successful despite aerial attacks, and on 1 March a further 16 merchant vessels carrying 6900 troops, as well as an air force contingent and supplies, left Rabaul and sailed north of New Britain in an attempt to deceive Allied Intelligence. But the convoy was sighted the next day off the western tip of New Britain entering the Vitiaz Strait and heading for Lae, which was only 100 miles away.

Fifth Air Force chief Gen Kenney decided to pull out all the stops, ordering the B-24-equipped 43rd Bomb Group to attack the convoy as soon as possible. This was the first day of an operation that would become known as the Battle of the Bismarck Sea, and the 49th FG would play an integral part during the opening 72 hours of the campaign.

On 3 March Allied air power was unleashed on the Japanese convoy. RAAF Beauforts and Beaufighters attacked at low altitude, while Fifth Air Force B-17s and B-24s bombed from high level and B-25 and A-20 strafers went in at wave-top height to attack the transports and escorting destroyers. Meanwhile, the 7th FS's P-40s dive-bombed and strafed the airfield at Lae. Lt A T House found himself right in the middle of the action, as he reported later;

'I was leading the second element with Maj Martin (squadron CO Jim Martin) as wingman. We were flying in string formation, losing altitude from 14,000 ft down to 9000 ft, where Capt McHale started his run to bomb Lae aerodrome. Anti-aircraft fire began just before Lt Benner started down, but it was not apparently firing at the dive-bombers but at the second element. The fire was heavy calibre, but scattered. Seemingly, it was ahead of us because of poor estimate of our speed. I started my run from 9000 ft, dropped to 6000 ft and then pulled up due to heavy AA, and Maj Martin did the same. I rolled over, continued the dive, released the bomb between 1200-1500 ft and continued south along the length of the runway, strafing.

'I then turned to the right and sighted a barge near the mouth of the Markham River. I fell in behind the flight leader, who made several passes, and on the second run fired five short bursts into the barge at short range. The barge was smoking and sinking. I pulled up to go over the trees and saw 11 unidentified aircraft at about 3000 to 4000 ft at "two o'clock". The aircraft were in elements of two, the second to the right and wide, making four-aeroplane flights.

'I did a gradual turn to the left and saw a single aircraft coming down from "ten o'clock". He started to fire at 2000 ft, and I started to call him on the radio, thinking he was one of our aeroplanes. As he fired, I glanced to the rear to see the whereabouts of Maj Martin, and saw enemy aircraft, one coming from "seven o'clock" and one from "four o'clock", both firing. I tried to turn inside the aeroplane approaching from "ten o'clock", pulling up into him for a head-on pass. I fired a long burst. His tracers were going behind me. My shots hit him right in the centre and the fighter exploded in mid-air.

'I stalled out, dropping my left wing. In the meantime, an enemy aircraft from "seven o'clock" had crossed to my left behind me, and I, turning left, came right into its course so that I could fire a long burst, which struck its motor and cockpit. The aircraft caught fire and continued down, falling into the water just offshore. During this combat, Maj Martin flew in the rear, diverting two enemy aircraft who were evidently approaching me from "six o'clock".'

Capt Ellis Wright led a formation of ten 8th FS P-40s flying cover for other Warhawks from his unit, as well as the 7th FS, which were dive-bombing the aerodrome at Lae. Sighting six Zeros flying at about 500 ft, he took his flight down to intercept. Wright opened fire and saw hits in the cockpit area of one of the Japanese fighters. It fell away immediately and crashed into the water. A few moments later he was on the tail of a second Zero. A good, solid burst stitched it from nose to cockpit, although Wright then lost sight of the Zero as he passed over it – his wingman saw it go into the water, however.

With a brief lull in the action, Wright took his flight up to 4000 ft, and as they manoeuvred they saw a staggered formation of four Zeros flying along the Markham River. Getting on the tail of the rearmost fighter in the formation, Wright fired from close range and his target exploded.

While the 49th FG's two P-40 squadrons continued their attacks on Lae, the P-38s of the 9th FS headed out to sea to escort the bombers sent to attack the troopships. Once overhead the vessels, they encountered Japanese fighters attempting to protect the transports, which were either badly damaged or sinking from repeated bombing attacks. One of those involved was Dick Bong, now returned from the 35th FG. He reported;

'Our flight was intercepted by seven "Oscars". In the ensuing engagement, I made a 45-degree deflection shot from above and behind and he started smoking. I made another pass at him just before he hit the water and crashed. While pulling up I saw another smoking Zero hit the water about a mile to my right. I made two more passes at an "Oscar" and started his gas tank leaking, but he kept going and I came home.'

The P-38 pilots were credited with seven enemy fighters destroyed for the day, with two probables. The 8th FS claimed six fighters shot down, while the 7th FS's bag was confined to House's two.

By 4 March the Japanese convoy was all but destroyed, A-20s and Australian Beaufighters continuing to shoot up the smoking ships, as well as enemy survivors on barges and in the water. P-38s of the 9th FS were sent out to escort these aircraft on their strafing missions over the shattered remnants of the convoy, as well as Lae, Malahang and Finschhafen. They met aerial opposition on several occasions, Lt Harry W Brown reporting;

'I was a member of a formation of 19 P-38s escorting A-20s and Beaufighters in a strafing mission to Lae Aerodrome. After completing this mission, we were proceeding to Finschhafen to accomplish a similar raid. About halfway between Lae and Finschhafen I sighted approximately 12 enemy fighters. I immediately attacked this formation. One aeroplane caught fire after the first pass. The second one I fired at snap-rolled and spun earthwards. This was after I saw my cannon tracers hit him immediately behind the cockpit. I lost sight of him when I attacked an aeroplane on a P-38's tail. I followed him, shooting, until I was beset by other aeroplanes.'

Lt John O'Neill was flying on Brown's wing, and he attacked the same formation. He picked the second fighter in the group and raked the length of the aircraft with cannon fire. It flipped over on its back and went down.

That same day the 7th FS escorted B-25s searching for surviving vessels from the convoy off Cape Ward Hunt. They found one stationary destroyer and watched the bombers score three direct hits. One flight then strafed the destroyer and a large number of barges and life-boats in the water – some of the small boats hastily mounted machine guns and returned the fighters' fire. The 8th FS also accompanied the bombers in searching for convoy remnants.

The group flew further mopping up operations on 5 March, and the 7th FS met 'Oscars' over Malahang during the course of one such mission. After a fierce fight which saw the Warhawks pursuing the Ki-43s in and out of the clouds, Capt Ray Melikian and Lts Donald Lee and Dave Baker all chalked up kills.

The 9th FS was also airborne, and its pilots ran into a scattered fighter formation over Lae.

P-40E *PISTOFF* was flown by the 7th FS's Lt Donald Lee during the Battle of the Bismarck Sea, downing an 'Oscar' with the machine on 5 March 1943 during attacks on the Japanese convoy which was destroyed in its attempt to reach Lae. He claimed three other victories during his tour with the 49th FG but fell one short of 'making ace' (*Steve Ferguson*)

It was, however, to be a triumphant, but near-fatal, combat for one group veteran. The 9th FS's Capt Bob Vaught downed two Zekes (to make him an ace), but then the left engine in his P-38G-15 failed and he was forced to head for home. Deciding to attempt a landing at Wau, he was on his final approach when the right engine quit and the aircraft hit the ground heavily, veering off the runway into some coffee trees.

When Vaught was removed from the wreckage he was declared dead by the Australian medic who had tried to revive him. However, as his canvas-wrapped body was being loaded onto a C-47 for removal to Port Moresby, the loaders were startled to hear a loud moan from the man who had been declared dead! The transport sped to Port Moresby, where Vaught was hospitalised and made a full recovery.

The three-day attack on the Japanese convoy during the Battle of the Bismarck Sea had cost the enemy dearly. Of the 7000 troops in the 18th Army contingent sent to reinforce Lae, over half had been lost – only 900 made it through. Japanese fleet destroyers managed to fish 2700 men from the sea and return them to Rabaul. A total of 14 merchant vessels and eight warships had been sunk, and 60 aircraft shot down – the 49th FG was credited with destroying 22 of the latter. Allied ground forces could now proceed with their ground offensive against Lae proper.

Lt Bob Vaught, seen here posing beside the nose of P-40E *BOB'S ROBIN* soon after moving to New Guinea from Darwin, was an early 49th FG scorer. He became an ace on 5 March 1943, but was almost killed in a forced landing shortly afterwards (*Author*)

DOBODURA DAYS

By early 1943 Col Bob Morrissey not only presided over Fifth Air Force's top-scoring group, but he had also been able to bring his three squadrons together at the newly built airfield at Dobodura, on the New Guinea coast. This was the first time that the 49th FG had operated from one base since its departure from the USA one year earlier. Here, squadron personnel would be able to brief together, share the same maintenance facilities and live in facilities where they could be as comfortable as was possible in New Guinea. It would be their home for the next seven months.

The 9th FS's P-38s were based on the south side of the Horanda runway, where they could taxi to the main strip and take off to the northeast. The 7th and 8th FSs were located just off the northern end of the shorter Kalamazoo runway, where their Warhawks could depart in pairs.

The 49th FG's newly built base at Dobodura, on the northeastern New Guinea coast, in mid 1943. The group saw much action from this base between March and November 1943 (*Steve Ferguson*)

8th FS Warhawks sit in the dispersal area alongside the shorter 'Kalamazoo' strip at Dobodura in the spring of 1943. The unit was operating rebuilt P-40Es when this photograph was taken (*Steve Ferguson*)

The P-38s scrambled early in the afternoon of 8 March to intercept nine 'Betty' bombers which had just attacked Oro Bay and were returning to their base at Gasmata, on New Britain. Capt Dick Taylor finally caught them at about 17,000 ft, but the P-38s continued to climb to 21,000 ft, which put them above the fleeing bombers.

At that point Taylor peeled off to the left to attack them head-on, sweeping below the G4Ms and firing at point blank range. The Lightning pilots made two more passes before being engaged by eight escorting 'Oscars', Taylor diving away and then returning, only to be challenged by two more Ki-43s. He set one of them on fire, before going after a 'Betty'. The bomber absorbed the full blast from the P-38's guns, began to smoke and started its long descent to the sea.

JAPANESE REVENGE

The Japanese sought revenge against the 49th FG on the 11th. Shortly before 1000 hrs a US Navy patrol vessel reported large formations of enemy aircraft headed towards Oro Bay. Group controllers immediately radioed the P-38 patrol led by Lt Tom Fowler, and scrambled the 8th and 9th FSs at Dobodura – Capt Larry Kirsch led the eight P-40s from the 8th while Capt Sid Woods headed a flight of four P-38s. The Japanese had turned out in force to strike Dobodura, with 24 'Betty' bombers, escorted by a similar number of Zekes, approaching from high altitude.

First contact was made by Lt Tom Fowler and his P-38s, which had climbed up-sun to attack from 23,000 ft. As the twin-engined fighters dived at the bombers, they were met head-on by three of the escorting Zekes. Fowler and his wingman, Lt Carl Planck, both opened fire. Fowler's opponent took a long burst and Planck raked his Zeke from nose to tail at point blank range. Both Lightning pilots then broke away, with the sole surviving Zeke going after Planck, who was forced into a headlong dive. Having lost his pursuer, Planck performed a 180-degree turn and then sighted a P-38 trailing smoke. He went to see if he could help.

The fighter was being flown by Lt Bill Hanning, who had become separated from his wingman after running into Zekes when they went after the bombers. He had set one of the enemy fighters on fire with a good deflection shot and then turned into a second, head-on. As they came at each other, Hanning's right wingtip sliced through the Zeke's cockpit. The P-38 pilot had managed to regain control, but as he attempted to head for home, another Zeke came after him, leaving Hanning with no choice but to fight.

Twice they met head-on, but the P-38 had already sustained too much damage. Its canopy collapsed and engines burning, Hanning was on the verge of bailing out when he was spotted by Planck. The latter could little by watch as his squadronmate managed to unbuckle himself and get high enough into the slipstream to be pulled from the cockpit. Hanning blacked out and came to floating in his Mae West in Oro Bay, from where he was rescued by the crew of a tug.

The Dobodura-based interceptors were still airborne when the 'Bettys' headed for home. Capt Woods, with Lts Jack Mankin and Dick Bong, caught the bombers about 30 miles off shore, making a pass along their right flank. Woods hit one of the bombers with sustained bursts, which were sufficient to send it down. But then the three P-38s were met by a large number of Zekes. Mankin managed to get away from his attackers, but as he attempted to chase the bombers, he encountered more Zekes, which he attacked. One stalled in a climbing turn and he managed to set it on fire, but the second gained an initial advantage, so Mankin rolled the Lightning over and dived away.

Bong had a very successful encounter. After nine Zekes had chased his flight away from the bombers, he tried to go back, but the enemy pursued him down to sea level. He later related;

'We were headed toward Gasmata. I flew straight until I could see only one Zero behind me. I made a 180-degree turn and put a long burst into the Zero head-on. Instead of one Zero there were nine or more, and I turned five-degrees left and put a short burst into another Zero head-on. Both of them had their belly tanks on. I then turned ten degrees right and put a long burst into another Zero from 20 degrees deflection, then I turned 20 degrees left to observe the results. The first two Zeros were burning all around the cockpit, and the third one was trailing a long column of smoke. Three Zeros split-essed down on me and shot up my left engine and wing while I was running home. I feathered the left engine and landed safely.'

After a long tail chase, the P-40s of the 8th FS finally caught the bombers some 75 miles out to sea. Lt Dan Moore said of their encounter;

'Lt (William) Day put his flight in position to make a pass at the bombers, which were out in front of the fighters. I was in the No 2 position. Lt Day and I made a pass at the rear bomber of the right wing. We both got in good shots, and pieces were seen flying off the right wing and fire coming from the engine. The bomber, when last seen, was losing altitude.

'We then went underneath the bombers and were turning to make another pass when the Zeros jumped us. We split up, and I saw a Zero diving on me in a head-on attack. I pulled up and began shooting straight at his engine. Flames began pouring out from the engine, and the last time I saw the aeroplane it was in a gentle turn, losing altitude at a rate of around 500 ft a minute.'

Moore was credited with the Zero and Day with a bomber and a fighter. Lt Clyde Barnett also downed one of the escorts.

Upon returning to Dobodura the pilots found that their base had suffered damage. More seriously, Sgt Frederick Bente had been killed running up his P-38, and several other personnel wounded – some seriously – when the 9th FS dispersal area suffered several direct hits. These were the first ground casualties that the 49th had suffered since its entry into the combat zone.

Throughout this period the Japanese continued to send high altitude reconnaissance aircraft out over Allied airfields on a near-daily basis. And although the 49th FG conducted routine patrols, interception was not always possible. But on 25 March Capt Bill Haney and Lt Ed Ball of the 9th FS were able to catch a lone 'Betty' heading for Dobodura at 24,000 ft. Ball made the first pass, silencing the tail gunner, followed by Haney. Both pilots then performed a series of independent passes on the G4M, but it continued on its way to Dobodura. Finally, Haney raked it from both sides at point blank range, after which the 'Betty' rolled over on its back and plunged seawards.

On the 28th there was another raid on Oro Bay, the Japanese sending a large force of aircraft which included 'Val' dive-bombers and some 40 to 50 fighters to attack shipping in the harbour. Both the 8th and 9th FSs saw considerable action, and although they were never able to reach the 'Bettys' that bombed from high altitude, there were some major dogfights. The P-38s and P-40s engaged the enemy almost simultaneously, and for 30 minutes the group pressed home its attacks. In the final reckoning the 9th FS was credited with six destroyed, while the 8th FS went one better with seven confirmed and four probables, including two 'Vals'. Only one P-40 (and its pilot) was lost in the encounter.

The following day the Lightning pilots pursued a reconnaissance aircraft, Clayton Barnes and Dick Bong finally catching the Mitsubishi Ki-46 'Dinah' over the Bismarck Sea. Bong hit its left engine on his first pass and the aircraft exploded after his fourth.

There was a lull in the action for the 49th FG for about a week, and other than the daily reconnaissance overflights, there were no Japanese raids. But things were about to change in a big way, for Adm Isoruko Yamamoto, Commander-in-Chief of the Japanese Combined Fleet, had assembled some 350 naval and army aircraft to prosecute his *I-Go* offensive. The 49th would be in action from the first day of the campaign – 11 April 1943 – when missions were directed against Oro Bay.

Maj Peaslee had a force of 15 P-38s patrolling over Dobodura at 24,000 ft when the alert came that the Japanese were on their way. However, for some strange reason Peaslee's flight was initially misdirected, leaving it orbiting out of range while the other elements – P-40s from the 7th and 8th FSs – attacked the enemy formation. The 9th's formation was led by Lt Clyde Harvey, who replaced Dick Bong when the latter was forced to abort with engine failure. Lt Theron Price reported what happened next;

'We turned towards Oro Bay and saw 12 to 15 "Oscars" at about 15,000 ft in a layer of clouds. The flight leader called our attention to them and headed in that direction. As we approached the enemy aircraft, an "Oscar" dived on Lt Harvey and Lt Holze's tail. I was out of range but fired a burst to scare him away. It worked and he pulled up. I fired another burst at one that ran through my sights. This burst was observed to hit, but did not seem to have any effect. Then I pulled up and fired at the other one until he definitely started smoking and burst into flames, and then went out of control.

'At that time I looked back just as three other "Oscars" got onto my tail, and one of them was firing at me. Several shots hit my aeroplane and one exploded in the cockpit. Shrapnel hit my face and left arm. I dived out and through the clouds, leaving the "Oscar" behind. I pulled out at about 7000 ft and saw an "Oscar" crash into the water behind and to the left, which I claim to be the one I shot at.'

Crew Chief Akin's P-38G *"KWICHERKICKEN"* was the aircraft assigned to Lt Theron 'Pappy' Price of the 9th FS. A senior lieutenant, he flew this machine from Dobodura until he was posted missing in action on the disastrous mission to Rabaul on 12 October 1943 (*Steve Ferguson*)

During that same engagement, Lt Ernest Harris led a flight of 8th FS P-40s over Oro Bay at 20,000 ft, and they bounced 15 Zekes 2000 ft below them. He fired a quick burst at a fighter from directly behind, and his wingman, Flt Off Sammy Pierce, saw pieces fly off it as the enemy aircraft burst into flames. Having dived down to 13,000 ft but found nothing, both P-40 pilots then climbed back up to 20,000 ft, from which height Harris spotted 'the dive-bombers attacking two ships out in the bay, but we weren't able to reach them'. He went on;

'We made a wide circle out to sea and saw an aeroplane burning on the water with a parachute near it. We then came back over the ships as 12 dive-bombers were making another run on them. I attacked two of the dive-bombers at a height of about 200 ft and saw one burst into flames and hit the water. Flt Off Pierce and I were then attacked by several Zekes and became separated. I hit one of the Zekes and saw him crash into the water. I also saw a Zeke which Capt Wright had shot down hit the water at about the same time. I circled for a while but was unable to sight any more of the enemy so I returned and landed.'

The Zeke Harris reported for Wright was one of three that the latter downed that day to 'make ace'.

The 7th FS also caught up with the dive-bombers over Oro Bay, and two of them were downed by Lts Robert Greene and Joseph O'Connor. Despite the 49th being credited with shooting down nine fighters and four dive-bombers on 11 April, the enemy would be back the next day. But before the bombing mission could begin again, a high altitude reconnaissance Ki-46 appeared over Dobodura which initiated a chase that would go on for some time.

Lt George Davis and wingmen Lts Merle Wolfe and Joel Thorvaldson were warned of an intruder, and they set off to find it. High above their base, they spotted the 'Dinah' flying at about 29,000 ft. When the Japanese pilot realised that he had been spotted, he continued to climb to 31,000 ft, confident that the Warhawks would be unable to follow him. But the chase continued all the way to Port Moresby, where Davis was finally able to bring his guns to bear as the four aircraft flew over Cape Ward Hunt.

Closing to 300 yards, he opened fire, and the Dinah's left engine burst into flames. Davis' guns then jammed not once, but twice, although he managed to get one operating and the Ki-46 finally slipped down trailing smoke. Davis then went home, where he belatedly received confirmation of his victory.

The 49th FG received new P-40N-5s in the summer of 1943, and 2Lt Sammy Pierce, seen here in his favourite baseball cap, was allotted 'Yellow 55'. Note the hand crank sticking out of the cowling to the left of Pierce. This was used to start the engine, as electric starters were omitted from early P-40Ns to save weight. Pierce's Warhawk was amongst the first batch of P-40Ns assigned to V Fighter Command in the summer of 1943, these aircraft being sent to New Guinea to replace ageing P-40E/Ks. He had already scored three confirmed victories by this time, and he flew this machine, which carried the name *HAILEAH WOLF* on the right side of the nose, for several months. Pierce did not claim any confirmed victories with it, however. After completing his first combat tour in May 1944, Pierce served briefly as a test pilot in the US before returning to the 8th FS. On 26 December 1944, he shot down four Japanese fighters to bring his final total to seven confirmed victories (*Author*)

The name *KAY – STRAWBERRY BLONDE* appeared on the port side of Flt Off Pierce's 'Yellow 42', shown here at Dobodura in the spring of 1943. Its worn appearance is typical of 49th FG Warhawks during this period. Sammy Pierce had graduated from flight training as a staff sergeant in one of the few NCO-only classes of the period (*Author*)

Lt Zappia of the 7th FS poses with his P-40 *BROOKLYN'S BAD BOY*. Zappia was typical of the many unsung fighter pilots of World War 2 who saw their share of the fighting but were never fortunate enough to score any aerial kills (*Steve Ferguson*)

ATTACK ON PORT MORESBY

Instead of returning to Oro Bay on the 12th, the enemy sent two formations of 18 'Bettys', along with a substantial fighter escort, to attack Port Moresby. Initial contact was made by the Lightnings of the 9th FS, the unit being led by Lt Ralph Wire and his No 2 Lt Grover Fanning, who was to enjoy a most successful day. The latter reported;

'We flew over the mountains to Port Moresby, reaching an altitude of 29,000 ft. Over Moresby, we dropped our belly tanks because we sighted the enemy off to our left. Lt Pete Alger led us in a beautiful pass at one of the bomber formations. I definitely saw two formations of 18 ships in each one, with lot of "Oscars" above the formations. We made our pass and came back from the other side for another one. This was a close pass, and I shot into the right engine of one "Betty" bomber. As it dived away in a left turn it was smoking.

'I then peeled away to the right and Lt Alger to the left, because the "Oscars" were coming down on us. After outrunning the "Oscars", I turned back towards the bombers and saw one going down in flames. I came back at the bomber formation from the right. I made a quarter head-on pass and reached the front of the bomber formation. Again I had to dive away from "Oscars". They were coming down mostly in threes.

'I then came back at the bomber that had dived out of formation, and made a diving pass as an "Oscar" was covering it. The bomber began to smoke. I believe I got the tail gunner because I passed right by the tail and there was no fire this time. Then I chased the bomber back over the mountains, heading 15 degrees. I caught up with the two after passing over the range. I had trouble getting into position for a pass because of the "Oscar". Finally, he got close to the bomber and I made a quarter tail pass. The "Oscar" moved to a position over the nose of the bomber.

'When I started firing, the bomber started a diving left turn. The "Oscar" went straight up, whipped over and went straight down – I managed to avoid going under him. I fired a good burst into the bomber as it started to dive away again. The bomber burst into flames along the right side of the fuselage at the wing roots.

'The "Oscar" was ahead of the bomber and above. He went up again, and I caught him at the top of his stall. I fired, apparently right into the nose and cockpit of the aeroplane. The "Oscar" fell off out of control and started smoking from both sides. It went into the low overcast, out of control, diving too low to the ground to pull out. Away to my left was a lone aeroplane, apparently a bomber in trouble. Still farther away was a flight of bombers. I started to investigate the lone ship, but was out of oxygen and was above 20,000 ft.'

The 8th FS caught the bombers near Cape Ward Hunt after their attack, the unit's pilots duly being credited with downing three 'Oscars' and two bombers in the encounter. The Japanese, however, had enjoyed some success by setting fuel dumps on fire and destroying several B-25s.

There was no action on the 13th, but the following day the Japanese assembled a large force of 27 'Betty' bombers and 'Val' dive-bombers, plus escorting fighters, to attack the harbour and airfield at Milne Bay, on the very eastern tip of New Guinea.

Because of the distances involved, the chances of successful interception were minimal, and only a few Lightnings (with better endurance than the

Unlike Zappia, Lt Martin 'Pete' Alger (seen here second from left, with his groundcrew) managed to claim four kills and a single probable during his tour with the 9th FS in 1943 (*Steve Ferguson*)

Lt Pete Alger's P-38G is serviced at one of the many dirt strips that were hastily created around Port Moresby in 1942-43. This photograph was taken on 12 April 1943 (*Steve Ferguson*)

P-40) from the 9th FS were involved. Two flights, led by Lt Bill Sells, ran into trouble from the beginning, and new flight leader Dick Bong lost half of his flight early on when two pilots aborted the mission through engine trouble, leaving only Bong and his wingman Carl Planck. Then Sells lost his wingman, reducing P-38 strength to five. To make matters worse, Sells had difficulty finding the enemy. He took his flight down from 26,000 ft while Bong and Planck stayed at altitude. The enemy arrived shortly after Sells' departure, as Bong reported;

'Planck and myself intercepted three waves of "Bettys" at 26,000 ft. Lt Planck had trouble with his engines and failed to get a shot. I made a pass from above and behind the last wave and shot one "Betty" on the left flank and set it on fire, as witnessed by Lt Planck. I hit another bomber in the second wave and saw no result. I passed under the first wave as they dropped their bombs. I had to leave with six black Zeros chasing me.

'I left them, and then turned back to make a pass at three "Betty" bombers. I hit the left wingman and started his left engine smoking. He left the formation and started down. Two Zeros jumped me and I had to dive to 5000 ft to get away and come home. The last Zero put a 20 mm cannon shell in my elevator. There were about 27 bombers and 15 or 20 black Zeros that I saw.'

While Bong was in combat with the 'Bettys', Sells and his two wingmen had intercepted the dive-bombers and fighters between 16,000 and 20,000 ft. Sells directed Lt Eddie Howes to go for the 'Vals' while he and Lt Ralph Hays took on the fighters. Howes dived into an echelon of dive-bombers, sprayed them with fire and scattered their formation. He wheeled around to attack another 'Val' but was set upon by the Zeros. Immediately, Howes was forced to break away and head for home. As he did, Howes saw a P-38 surrounded by a dozen or so enemy fighters. He

1Lts Walter Markey (left) and Dick Bong study combat reports in their tent at Dobodura in the autumn of 1943. Markey became a 9th FS flight leader and finished his tour with four confirmed victories and one probable to his name (*Steve Ferguson*)

did his best to aid its pilot by firing at one Zero, but was then forced to break off.

Sells and Hays had taken on a hopeless quest. They soon became separated, and Hays managed to rake a couple of 'Vals' before the Zeros forced him to use his superior speed to quit. This left Sells to take on the Zeros alone, and despite his P-38 being riddled with bullets, he somehow emerged from the battle unhurt. Escaping into the clouds, he made it to the RAAF airfield at Gurney Field, near Milne Bay, but as he attempted a landing, an Australian Warhawk dropped into the landing pattern directly in front of him. Sells pulled up to avoid a collision, crashed into the trees and was killed.

AFTER *I-GO*

Following this series of heavy losses to both his fighter and bomber units, Yamamoto ordered the cancellation of Operation *I-Go*. In an effort to bolster flagging morale, he prepared to make an inspection trip of bases in the Solomon Islands on 18 April. As he departed on the first leg of his flight, Yamamoto was unaware that the Japanese code had been broken, and that his 'Betty' would be intercepted by P-38s based at Henderson Field, Guadalcanal. The master tactician who had been a thorn in American sides since Pearl Harbor was removed from the scene for good.

Still reeling from Yamamoto's loss, Japanese bombers went on the attack once again on 14 May when they targeted Allied shipping in Oro Bay with 18 'Bettys', escorted by over 30 Zeros. The 49th FG was alerted early, and the initial interception came about when a high altitude reconnaissance aircraft arrived over Cape Ward Hunt. A flight of P-38s was scrambled, and Lt Martin 'Pete' Alger sighted the intruder heading for Oro Bay. He later stated;

The 7th FS's Lt Don Lee poses with his P-40E at Dobodura in May 1943 – he would receive a brand new P-40N soon after this photograph was taken. The aircraft's name probably sums up the attitude of most servicemen in the Pacific at that time. Note the fighter's wheel hub decoration (*Author*)

7th FS pilots pose for the camera at Waigani (17-Mile) strip in New Guinea in 1943. They are, from left to right, Hale, Dillworth, King, Lucius LaCroix, Arland Stanton, Clyde Knisley, Paul Slocum, David Baker and McDaris, sat atop John Yancey's P-40E (*Author*)

'I saw the enemy aeroplane at "nine o'clock" at about 28,000 ft. I called Lt Finberg and told him the position, but he could not see it, so he told me to chase it. I turned toward the enemy and gave chase. I was indicating 250 mph at 28,000 ft, and caught him after about five minutes. I made an attack from the left rear and set the left engine alight. I passed under him and turned back for a rear attack from the right. On this pass I set his right

engine smoking. I then sat behind him and continued to fire until he blew up, the aircraft continuing to burn all the way down. I saw one half-opened parachute following the flaming ship, and it hit the water about 100 yards behind the bomber. I claim one enemy bomber, type "Dinah".'

Within the next hour the bombers, and their escorts, arrived to find a 49th FG 'reception committee'. Capt John M Yancey was leading the 7th FS's 'Yellow Flight' at 23,000 ft when the enemy was sighted. Following 'Red Flight' into the bombers, Yancey singled out a smoking 'Betty' at the rear of the formation and made a pass from '11 o'clock'. His cone of fire raked the whole length of the bomber and his second element leader saw it in flames. Yancey continued in a shallow glide, climbed left and opened fire, then banked left and encountered a Zero.

He then dived to 14,000 ft and sighted another fighter to the left, and above, the bombers, heading north. Before he was seen, Yancey fired and the fighter immediately burst into flames, with black smoke pouring out of it. Seeing another Zero above, he rolled over and dived out. He pulled back up, sighted two more Zeros and a P-38 in combat and attempted to help his countryman, but the Lightning went down. Yancey immediately encountered yet another Zero and dived away towards the coast.

It was at this point that the 'Eightballs' in their war-weary P-40Es (each of which had about 300 combat hours on them) now entered the fight, and they were to enjoy their greatest triumph of the war. Veteran Lt Ernest Harris led his flight into the bombers in a frontal pass, firing a long burst into the left wing of one which was seen by his wingman to crash into the water. Harris then turned into another 'Betty', raking it from stem to stern until his guns were empty. He and his wingmen saw three bombers in the water, including a 'Betty' with its crew members clustered on the wing.

Lt Richard Vodra also had a good day after his flight made contact at 20,000 ft. He reported;

Capt Bob White of the 8th FS shows the victory markings after his Oro Bay successes (a Zeke kill and a 'Betty' probable) in P-40E-1 41-25174 which have him ace status on 14 May 1943. White left his home in Kansas City, Missouri, to join the USAAC as an aviation cadet just five days after the attack on Pearl Harbor. He was posted to the 8th FS in late 1942 and scored his first five victories between 7 January and 14 May 1943 to join the group's growing list of aces. During the 14 May interception at Oro Bay, White scored one of 13 victories credited to the 8th FS – a feat which earned the squadron the first Distinguished Unit Citation to be awarded to an individual squadron during World War 2 (*Steve Ferguson*)

'I was forced to drop back from the flight as my aeroplane seemed to lose power, but was able to complete two passes at the bombers before I was attacked by two Zeros and forced to dive out. On my way down, diving away from the two Zeros, two more entered in the chase by using a front quarterly attack from above me. I pulled into them and one turned away, offering a non-deflection shot. The Zero started smoking and later burst into flames, crashing on the shore a few miles south of Oro Bay.

'Several members of our groundcrew witnessed the Zero in flames and saw it crash. I then pulled out at 10,000 ft and began my climb. At about 15,000 ft I saw a dogfight going on out to sea, and after reaching it saw a lone P-40 with a Zero on his tail. After expending the remainder of my ammunition at him, the Zero pulled up abruptly, snap-rolled and started to descend. Lt Harrison of the 7th FS, who was flying the P-40 being chased by the Zero, saw it burst into flames and crash in the water.'

The day's last combats took place as the P-38s of the 9th FS chased the bombers out to sea, although the latter were still being stoutly defended by many Zeros. Lt Keith Oveson was the only member of his flight to reach the enemy as they fled. He reported;

'We made interception of enemy bombers escorted by Zero fighters. We came upon them from the rear and left. We outran them and turned

Lt John Griffith's 7th FS P-40K *Vera* made a wheels-up landing following the Oro Bay clash on 14 May 1943. The fighter's spinner was painted light blue *(Steve Ferguson)*

Lt Hilliard's P-40K looks resplendent with its new star and bar national marking and high visibility tail surfaces. These markings were added to all 7th FS machines following a directive from Fifth Air Force HQ in the summer of 1943. The fighter's blue spinner represented the 7th's squadron marking within the 49th FG *(Steve Ferguson)*

to the right to make a head-on attack. As I went into make my pass, I was attacked by Zeros from below and above. I skidded out of their line of fire, then, as I straightened out, I put a burst into the lead bomber of the extreme outside "V". I then put two bursts into the left wing man. Smoke appeared out of the left engine and I dove out.

'As I went under the bombers, I was attacked by three or four Zeros individually. I continued my dive and met a Zero coming in on a quartering shot from the right. He was so close that all I could do was pull up and rake him from nose to tail. I observed no results as I had to duck to keep from ramming him. I saw the pilot clearly, and noticed that the grey paint along the fighter's fuselage was chipped, as was the red circle, leaving only about three-fourths of it intact. Lt Sutliff of the 7th FS saw this aeroplane crash into the water.

'I continued my dive, chased by Zeros, for about 2000 to 3000 ft at approximately 450 to 475 mph. Having distanced them, I started my climb back up. I then noticed an aeroplane burning on the sea below me, which was the "Betty" bomber I had shot a minute before. This was confirmed by my wingman, who was following me on the pass.'

Total claims for the day were eleven bombers and ten fighters, with the 'Eightballs' accounting for seven and six respectively.

COMBAT OVER BENA BENA

Forced to make good the losses suffered during Operation *I-Go*, the Japanese transferred in a Ki-43-equipped *sentai* from Indo-China, together with further reinforcements in the formidable form of the in-line engined Kawasaki Ki-61 ' Tony'. Other new arrivals included more Ki-48 twin-engined 'Lily' medium bombers and Nakajima Ki-49 'Helen' heavy bomber.

Having helped defeat *I-Go*, the 49th returned to offensive operations escorting bombers, as well as flying patrols over Allied bases in New Guinea. Then, on 12 June, 12 9th FS P-38s were sent to escort C-47s carrying supplies to the Australian forward base at Bena Bena. On their return, the Lightning pilots encountered 15 'Oscars' at 11,000 ft about ten miles south-east of Bena Bena. The two-ship flight of Woods wasted no time in engaging the enemy, as Bong reported;

'I saw eight "Oscars". We were at 11,000 ft, with the enemy at 14,000 ft. The enemy peeled off on Blue flight, which was the second flight. I went into the attack against five "Oscars", which were attacking Blue flight. I got one 90-degree deflection shot with no observed results. I then dove through a cloud layer to lose three "Oscars" that were on my tail. I went straight on out and climbed to 12,000 ft, before turning back into seven or eight of them. They were below me, and about a mile away. I picked out one that was flying toward me and attacked him head-on, opening fire at about 600 yards and continuing to about 50 yards. I hit him, but saw no results. I had to dive out again because of "Oscars" on my tail. I then climbed back to 8000 ft and saw three at the same altitude at "12 o'clock". I made another head-on attack.

'Just before opening fire, one made a slight turn to the left and I aimed at him. I made a long burst, ten degrees deflection, at 200 yards. There were two explosions in his aeroplane. After passing him, I looked back over my shoulder and saw him going vertically down in a slight turn to the left. I looked in front and saw another "Oscar" coming across my flight path at about 45 degrees. I took a shot at him with no known results. I looked back at the "Oscar", which I claim, and he was still going straight down in a semi-spin, and was only about 1000 ft from the ground. Upon reaching base I found they had shot my right tyre flat, I had two holes in each wing and the hydraulic system out. By using the hand pump I got the wheels down.'

Clayton Barnes also got one of the 'Oscars' when he caught it in a stall at the top of its loop.

On 30 June Lt Col Bob Morrissey was transferred to Fifth Air Force Headquarters, and he was succeeded as group CO by Maj James Selman. In other changes, the 475th FG was formed around a core of veteran pilots transferred in from the 49th FG. Some of these men had chosen to volunteer for service with the new group when they realised that it would be exclusively flying the P-38 – equipment many old 49th hands had been awaiting for some time. Others switched groups because they felt that they would stand a better chance of promotion in the 475th FG.

A series of uneventful escort missions were flown until the 9th FS saw action on 3 July. P-38s had accompanied C-47s to Mubo, and on their return to base they had caught 'Lily' bombers in the middle of an attack. Someone shouted 'Enemy aircraft at "six o'clock" over the intercom, and Lt Carl Aubrey reacted instinctively to the call. He reported;

'I continued until I saw an unidentified bomber and two Zekes about 3000 ft below us. I dropped my belly tank and made a pass at the middle Zeke. My pass was okay, but I was firing too far behind because of my high speed. I chandelled sharply to the right. When I got straightened out, I saw a Zeke flying about 35 degrees off to my left, and slightly below. I finally closed on him and gave him a long burst. He took no evasive action but simply burst into flames and spun into the sea off Salus Lake. I also saw a Zeke trailing flames fall into Salus Lake, and a second machine hit the shore near the lake. I later learned that the one which went in burning was downed by Lt Elliott Dent and the other one by Lt Sheldon Brinson.'

One other Zeke was downed by Lt Owen Swartz, while Lt George McMurry attacked an element of bombers, and on his second pass a 'Lily' began to blaze and eventually crashed into the sea.

On 8 July eight P-38s of the 9th FS were again escorting C-47s to Bena Bena when several Zekes appeared. Lt Ralph Hays made several passes at

Capt Sheldon Brinson of the 7th FS was a flight leader throughout 1943, during which time he claimed two kills in two combats, although only one was subsequently confirmed. His total score was three confirmed and two probables (*Steve Ferguson*)

different fighters, but all broke off combat. Hays finally headed for two that were on the tail of a P-38, and although they fled, he was finally able to get a good tail shot at one of them. The fighter half-rolled and went down in a vertical spiral. It was last seen going into haze at mountain top height.

Two days later, while on patrol over Wau and Salamaua, the 9th FS jumped a large formation of Zekes. Capt Thomas Fowler got one, but not before Flt Off Archie Davis had been shot down. Both Fowler and Lt Leroy Donnell also sustained damaging hits.

The 7th FS was back in action on the 14th while escorting transports in the Salamaua area, the P-40 pilots jumping a formation of 'Val' dive-bombers and downing three of them. One fell to a recently arrived replacement pilot whose name would become well known in the squadron – Lt Bob DeHaven. Following his first combat, he reported;

Future ranking P-40 ace Bob DeHaven flew his P-40N as 'White 13' during the autumn of 1943. It was rebuilt at Gusap in February-March 1944 and then reassigned to the 8th FS/49th FG as 'Yellow 67'. The name *Rita* on the starboard cowling (together with the seven kill flags on the port side of the fuselage) was carried over from DeHaven's days, but the yellow number and yellow/black/yellow spinner are 8th FS markings. It is seen here soon after arriving at Cyclops Field, Hollandia, in May 1944, the fighter carrying three drop tanks following its long flight from Gusap (*Steve Ferguson*)

1Lt Ralph Wandrey (second from left) claimed six kills with the 9th FS during his 16-month combat tour, which ran from 1 April 1943 through to August 1944. Completing 191 combat missions in that time, he scored five kills with the P-38 and a solitary victory with the P-47 (*John Stanaway*)

'I identified the ship as a type 99 ("Val") dive-bomber. As I started my first pass from the right, the enemy started a slight turn to the left, enabling me to get approximately a one-second burst in which evidently killed the rear gunner, as he didn't fire thereafter. I crossed to his left side and he continued his turn to the left. I followed him in his turn, expending at least a four-second burst. Just after I started firing on the second pass he started smoking, and I broke away so close that I could distinguish his tail number. I was preparing to make another pass when he started a slow wing over to the left and went into the water.'

But the 9th FS lost an aircraft and nearly its pilot. On his first pass, Lt Donald Lee was hit by the 'Val's' rear gunner and his coolant system damaged. He was forced to bail out about two-and-a-half miles from Lasanga Island and found that he could not inflate his life-raft when he landed in th water. Capt Ray Melikian was not about to abandon him, so he instructed other pilots to drop their rafts and then orbit the site while Lt Lucius Lacroix strafed marauding sharks. When the P-38 pilots ran low on fuel, some 8th FS pilots took over the watch until A-20s came along and dropped a big raft into which Lee was able to clamber. A broken arm hindered his rowing, but he was finally rescued and taken to Oro Bay.

The 9th FS escorted Martin B-26 bombers on a mission to Lae on the 23rd, and during the course of the mission several 'Oscars' put in an appearance. One was downed by Lt Ralph Wandrey and another by Lt Charles Ralph, while three more were probably destroyed. One of the latter was credited to another new name that would soon become synonymous with the 49th FG – Lt Gerald R Johnson.

When a dozen P-38 pilots took off on a scramble to Salamaua three days later, they could not know what lay ahead for them. Two aircraft aborted, and as the remaining ten were probing the Markham Valley on their way to Lae, some 20 enemy fighters suddenly appeared – both Zekes and 'Tonys'. Lt Dick Bong enjoyed his best day, later reporting;

'We went down the Markham Valley just to the back of Lae at 16,000 ft. On our way there I called in aeroplanes at "12 o'clock", and we were intercepted at 1350 hrs over the Markham Valley. There were about 20 fighters. I dropped my tanks and shot at an inline (engine) job and missed. I dove out and shot at a Zeke head-on, and he burst into flames. I shot at an inline job 45 degrees from behind and above and knocked pieces off his fuselage. I shot at another inline job and he burst into flames. I shot at another Zeke head-on and knocked pieces out of his canopy and engine cowling or engine. I shot at one more inline job and missed. I left the area at 1410 hrs.'

Bong had just downed four enemy aircraft in a single engagement. Now a triple ace with 15 victories, it was becoming almost matter-of-fact for him. The group's history observed, 'He would describe a major engagement in the same amount of space another man would take to tell of drinking three beers'. Fellow Lightning pilot Capt James A 'Duckbutt'

The first Lightning assigned to Jerry Johnson after his arrival in New Guinea was P-38F-5 42-12655, which he named *"SOONER"* and had numbered 'White 83'. This machine was written off on 26 July 1943 when its lower left tail section was ripped away by a mortally damaged Ki-61 which Johnson had just hit with cannon and machine gun fire during a head-on attack over Salamaua. Minutes earlier he had claimed his first official kill when he destroyed a Ki-43 over Markham Valley. Johnson struggled back to Horanda Strip, escorted by three P-39s from the 39th FS. '83' was subsequently 'scrapped out' (*John Stanaway*)

Capt James Watkins and P-38G-10 42-12882 *Charlcie Jeanne* were photographed shortly after the former had scored the last kills of his first combat tour in 1943. Watkins claimed a stunning ten victories in three missions over the space of a week – four on 26 July, three on 28 July and three on 2 August (*Steve Ferguson*)

Watkins had not enjoyed the same success as Bong during his lengthy tour, and he was now just a matter of days away from returning home after serving for almost a year with the 49th. To date, he had just one kill to his name, and his greatest wish was to score again before he left. Like Bong, Watkins found himself in the thick of the action on 26 July;

'I turned my flight into the attack at the rear after dropping belly tanks. Two inline aircraft were coming down head-on. I shot the first one and observed the canopy come off and the pilot jumped out as the ship rolled over. This ship was observed to catch fire, and this was confirmed by Lt Gerald R Johnson, who was flying on my wing. I immediately climbed into the overcast and came out again. I saw two Type IIIs ("Tonys") diving head-on at a P-38 ("White 83", piloted by Johnson). The P-38 shot down the first one, and the second turned into me. I started firing at a 45-degree angle, head-on from above. He caught fire from the engine on back, rolled over and went straight in from 9000 ft.

'While turning to observe this aeroplane, two other enemy fighters came at me head-on. I started firing at the first, which was about 500 yards ahead of the second. The first one burst into flames as he passed under me, and I clipped a short burst at the second one. No results were observed.

'I tried to break off further engagements but saw a single enemy aeroplane at a distance, and fired a long burst at him from about 1000 to 1500 yards. Naturally, there were no results. I climbed back to 10,000 ft, right into the middle of the dogfights, and levelled off. I saw a Type III fighter directly in front at about 2000 yards. He turned to the left and I

Soon to take command of the 9th FS, Capt Johnson points out one of the names which adorned P-38G-10 42-12882 of 11-kill ace Capt James 'Duckbutt' Watkins. This photograph was taken at Horanda strip in early August 1943 (*John Stanaway*)

turned inside him and shot him from the rear and above after a 180-degree turn. The aeroplane whipped over to the right and went into a spin. I observed no smoke or flames. The enemy aircraft was still spinning at about 4000 ft when I left. I believe the pilot was killed.'

Lt Gerald Johnson also scored his first victories during this huge dogfight, destroying a Zeke and shooting a 'Tony' off Watkins' tail.

Watkins had another good day on the 28th when nine P-38s took off to escort B-25s to Rein Bay, on New Britain. He reported;

'We were at 6000 ft when we sighted 12 to 18 fighters 3000 ft above us off Cape Raoult at 0815 hrs. We dropped our belly tanks and the flight turned 90 degrees into the attack. I fired at the leader and missed. I climbed to 8000 ft out at sea and made a head-on attack at one of two "Oscars" attacking Lt Bong. The aeroplane burst into flames about 75 to

P-38H-1 '83' (serial unknown, furthest from the camera) was inherited by Jerry Johnson when he replaced Maj Sid Woods as CO of the 9th FS in August 1943. Note the aircraft's old style national markings. It was marked as aircraft '92' when assigned to Woods (*John Stanaway*)

Capt Jim Watkins thought he was going home with only a single kill to his credit as his combat tour neared its end in the late summer of 1943. However, in just three missions his score rose from one to eleven – hence his smile in this official USAAF photograph, taken in August 1943. He would return to the 49th FG in late February 1945, adding one more kill before VJ-Day (*Author*)

100 yards in front of me. I turned to find Lt Bong, and made a head-on attack on one of three "Oscars" coming down on me. The ship burst into flames and pieces of it barely missed me as the fighter passed under my P-38. The others didn't bother me. I returned to the fight in a steep dive.

'At 4000 ft I levelled out to meet a head-on attack from two "Oscars". Neither would meet me, with the lead ship pulling straight up into a stall at about 6000 ft. I fired a long two- or three-second burst into him while he was hanging on his prop, and he went straight into the sea, exploding as he hit. I got in several more short bursts at others, but was chased off.'

Bong dived away from an attack by two 'Oscars' and then climbed back up to 8000 ft, before making head-on passes at two more. He achieved no

Well worn 9th FS P-38G/Hs are prepared for their next mission at Dobodura in August 1943. 'White 88' was assigned to Capt Clay Tice, 'White 95' was Capt Bill Haney's fighter (note its flight leader stripes), 'White 85' was flown by Capt Larry Smith and 'White 84' was Capt Jim Watkins' mount (*Steve Ferguson*)

result. He then peeled off to join five other P-38s, and was jumped by an enemy fighter, which put five shots into his aircraft. Bong then dived again to shake off his pursuer, after which he spotted two 'Oscars' attacking the B-25s. He immediately opened fire with a 45-degree deflection shot at one of the Ki-43s from the rear and above, continuing to press home his attack until the fighter almost turned into him. The long burst was effective, as the 'Oscar' slipped away on one wing and crashed.

Maj Sid Woods, Capt Bill Haney and Lt Ralph Wandrey were also credited with shooting down Ki-43s, but the day belonged to Watkins, who returned to Dobodura as a seven-victory ace.

NEW EQUIPMENT

The most noteworthy event for the 7th FS during mid 1943 was its re-equipment with new P-40Ns in place of the unit's by now war-weary E-models. Although eager to try them out in combat, the unit would have to wait several weeks before engaging the enemy once again.

Instead, the 9th FS found itself in the thick of the action again on 2 August while escorting B-25s on a strafing mission. Capt Larry Smith led the squadron, with the formidable trio of Capts Gerald Johnson, Wallace Jordan and James A Watkins as his flight leaders. It would be an action-filled mission, with a total of 11 'Oscars' being claimed destroyed for no loss.

The Lightnings had met 12 to 14 'Oscars' off Teliaga Point while the B-25s were sinking small boats and shooting up barges. Jim Watkins had quickly got into his stride, making a head-on pass at one of the Ki-43s, which was trying to climb out of the fight. Pieces flew off its canopy and wing, and the aircraft went straight down. A second was attacked as it tried to shoot down a B-25, Watkins again firing from head-on until the enemy fighter began to smoke. It hit the water from a height of 1500 ft. The Lightning ace then set off after a lone 'Oscar', catching it with a long burst as it attempted to turn to the right. The Ki-43 crashed into the water from about 300 ft. The man who thought he was going to have to go home without an official victory was now a double ace!

In the meantime Capt Johnson had lined up on two different 'Oscars', but when he pressed the trigger nothing happened. As he continued to manoeuvre, he saw three Ki-43s go into the water – all victims of his squadronmates. A very frustrated Johnson returned to base, where he discovered a blown fuse in his gun circuit. Besides Watkins, victories were scored by Wallace Jordan and Larry Smith and Lts Stanley Johnson, Francis Nutter, Grover Fanning, James Harris, George Alber and Frank Wunder.

July and August 1943 saw further personnel changes take place within the group, with many 9th FS veterans completing their combat tours and leaving for home. This left Gerald Johnson as the most senior captain within the unit, and he became the CO on 27 August when Maj Sid Woods shipped out. The previous month, ex-9th FS CO Col John C Selman had been appointed group commander. The final command change took place in late August when Capt Ray Melikian became CO of the 7th FS, which had by then been moved to a new airfield immediately christened 'Muddy Marilinan'. It was now indeed the rainy season, and there was little action for the group as a whole during August 1943.

On 2 September, however, 15 9th FS P-38s were given the task of escorting B-17s and B-26s sent to attack Cape Gloucester. The B-26s hastily unloaded their bombs and turned for home, but the B-17s hung around in the target area for some 45 minutes. As the P-38s continued to sweep the area, Johnson sighted five or six enemy aircraft preparing to pounce. One was a twin-engined fighter, as Johnson reported;

'I called the flight to drop belly tanks and turned to attack a twin-engined aeroplane that had just finished a pass at a B-17. I saw a P-38 take a snap shot at him. I attacked from above and behind, observing my fire hit around the engines and cockpit. He was smoking heavily as he rolled over and went into the sea. Lt Grover Fanning saw him burning in the water.

'I saw another twin-engined fighter attacking a B-17 and headed for him. Lt Theron D Price beat me there and fired a long burst from astern. I was unable to get a shot at this ship, but saw him diving away with his left engine smoking heavily, probably damaged by Lt Price's fire. I followed Lt Price while he chased a twin-engined fighter to Brogen Bay, and we both had deflection shots. I came up behind and fired at point blank range into his fuselage, but had to pull up to avoid over-running him. This aeroplane made a fight of it, turning and spiralling towards the water. He was then about 1000 ft high. Lt Price came in behind and nailed him. The twin-engined fighter hit the trees at about Cape Gauffre and burned.'

Just how many of these Japanese fighters were actually shot down has never been determined, but five official confirmations were granted, two of them to Fanning. The US pilots had encountered the two-seat Kawasaki Ki-45 'Nick' heavy fighter for the first time, this machine having originally been designed as a bomber-destroyer, with a 20 mm nose

Sgts Akins and Lynd clown around in front of Capt Dick Bong's P-38 shortly before it crashed whilst landing at Marilinan on 6 September 1943 (*Steve Ferguson*)

gun and a 37 mm forward-firing belly gun. The aircraft also possessed a light machine gun in the tail for rear defence.

HUON GULF OFFENSIVE OPENS

The Huon Gulf offensive started north of Lae and west of Hopoi on 4 September. Between 700 and 1000 Allied troops waded ashore, while paratroopers were landed in the Nadzab area, cutting off an escape route for the Japanese up the Markham Valley. The 49th FG was tasked with providing support for the troop transports but encountered no opposition, although the enemy arrived in strength after they had returned to base.

There was some compensation on the 6th when the 9th FS were patrolling the beachhead later that day, Capt Ralph Wire intercepting two Vs of nine 'Bettys' at about 15,000 ft, some 20 miles southeast of Lae. The first formation was unescorted, and about 15 miles ahead of the second, which was covered by 10 to 15 fighters. Wire submitted the following report;

'I was climbing for altitude to attack bombers when inline (engine) fighters made rear attack on my No 4 pilot, Lt Alber. I turned and met a fighter head-on, observing hits on its engine and cockpit. I last saw the fighter going straight down, smoking at about 7000 ft. I then turned to attack the second bomber flight of "Bettys", making a quarter head-on attack. I observed hits on its right engine and wing. The "Betty" started smoking heavily and lost altitude to the right. It was last seen by Lt Price at 4000 ft smoking and losing altitude rapidly.

'As I closed on the bombers for a second pass, I was attacked by four Zekes. I shot one down in flames, the Zeke being observed burning by Lt Karhausen. I then turned towards the bomber flight that was ten miles ahead. When I was about two miles from bombers, which were at 6000 ft and diving toward the ocean, I observed a Zeke coming up under my left wing. I climbed rapidly and the Zeke stalled and started to dive out. I then attacked it from the rear and observed hits around its cockpit. The Zeke hit the water out of control and exploded.'

Having just returned from a short leave, Dick Bong was also on this mission, but it was nearly his last. He made two passes at the bombers and scored numerous hits, leaving them smoking. He then noticed smoke coming from his own right engine. Bong cut it, feathered the propeller and headed for Marilinan. There, he found that his P-38 had suffered more damage than he had imagined – his right engine, right tyre and rudder trim tabs were all shot up, and on landing he crashed. To make matters worse, Bong's claims were downgraded to probables.

The 8th FS also attacked the 'Bettys', Lt Robert White downing two G4Ms and a Ki-61. He had positioned his flight ahead of the bombers and then turned for a 60-

Capt Dick Bong's P-38H-1 lies forlornly in a ditch at Marilinan after he lost power whilst coming in to land on 6 September 1943. His machine had been damaged by defensive fire from two 'Bettys' that he had attacked over Morobe. Despite seeing the bombers trailing smoke after his attacks, Bong was only credited with two probables. His Lightning, however, was declared a write-off after this incident (*Steve Ferguson*)

8th FS pilots stand in front of Lt Sammy Pierce's P-40N at Dobodura in August 1943. They are, from left to right, Hays, Drier, Carter, Flack, Sawyer and Talmadge (*Steve Ferguson*)

degree frontal attack, getting a good burst into the second bomber in the formation, which immediately dropped away – his wingman saw it crash into the sea near Tami Island. White made another pass down the side of the formation before pulling up for a head-on attack from beneath. A long burst caused a second 'Betty' to fall away out of control, the bomber only just missing him on the way down. Then, as White pulled up, he encountered a 'Tony' in front of him, and he swiftly shot its wing off. He had succeeded in scoring three of the 'Eightballs'' tally of four kills for this mission.

The 7th FS scrambled on 7 September, but only one pilot saw any action. Lt David Harbor was unable to climb to altitude due to trouble with his oxygen system, so he stayed at around 8000 ft. A short while later he sighted some B-25s below him, with two unidentified aircraft heading in their direction. Although he was able to identify them as 'Oscars', the enemy pilots had evidently not seen him.

Harbor pulled in behind one of the fighters and fired a 45-degree deflection shot. The enemy pilot flew straight into his fire and crashed onto the beach below. The P-40 pilot then chased the second 'Oscar', but soon found himself being shot at by the Lae aerodrome defences. Intense fire caused Harbor to break off and go home. With no witnesses, his claim was not allowed.

The 'Eightballs' next action took place over Hopoi in the late afternoon of 21 September. Led by their CO, Capt Ernest Harris, the P-40 pilots were returning from patrol when they were informed that Japanese bombers had been detected over Lae. They soon sighted 12 to 15 'Bettys', protected by a large, loose formation of escorts. The fight was on. One of the day's more successful pilots was Lt Harold Sawyer, who reported;

'Our flight climbed to 18,000 ft in an attempt to reach the bogies. We sighted two "Haps" (also known as Zeke 32s or "Hamps", which were all reporting names for the Mitsubishi A6M3) and the first element peeled off to the right to attack them. Lt David and I took one and started to follow him. I put a short burst into the "Hap" and he chandelled to the left and I closed in with a two- or three-second burst. He started smoking and going down, and I got on his tail and let him have another burst. He immediately burst into flames and went into a steep dive, turning to the right.

'I pulled up and started for home when I saw a three-ship high to my right. I pulled up from a "two o'clock" position and saw they were "Betty" bombers. I fired a long burst at the lead ship, hitting his nose and right engine. Smoke came from the engine first, and then it started to burn. I then dragged my fire through the left wing of the bomber, rolled over and came home.'

Lt John Hanson accounted for two 'Bettys' and damaged a third, as the squadron, all told, claimed ten aircraft destroyed for the loss of the P-40 flown by Lt Roger Grant. The latter had just accounted for a 'Hap' when he himself was hit by cannon fire from one of the bombers and forced to bail out. Grant languished in the jungle for 15 days before managing to return to Allied-controlled territory after a difficult and dangerous time evading capture.

FINSCHHAFEN INVADED

There were no further encounters with Japanese aircraft until the invasion of Finschhafen on 22 September 1943. The Australian troops sent in to take the strategically placed town on the northern New Guinea coast enjoyed massive fighter cover. The Japanese were fully aware of this, and they made only one small probing attack, which was repulsed by the 9th FS. The P-38 pilots succeeded in downing three of the six 'Oscars' they engaged, one of these falling to Capt Ralph Wire. His opponent proved very difficult to force down, as he recounted in his post-mission combat report;

'I made a tail attack on an "Oscar" at 1000 ft. He manoeuvred sharply to the right in an Immelman roll, then he did a split-ess back down to the water. I made four similar attacks and observed hits on the fuselage in each attack. After my fourth I saw the enemy fighter going down vertically from 1000 ft.'

The group kept itself busy flying the usual patrols over the beach for the rest of the month, but little opposition was encountered by the 49th. Indeed, only one victory was scored during the rest of September. This fell to Lt William Bleecker after his flight had spotted a lone 'Tony' in the Wewak area. The four P-38s, led by Capt Dick Bong, made hard work of the kill, however, despite the Japanese pilot performing a lazy loop which gave Bong and his wingman a chance to claim the victory. It finally

A seemingly war weary Capt Dick Bong poses with his P-38H-5 42-66847, which was issued to him as a replacement for the Lightning he had written off on 6 September. This photograph was taken at the end of the Rabaul offensive in November 1943, at which point Bong's tally stood at 21 – he had claimed his final kills of 1943 on 5 November (two Zekes over Rabaul) (*Steve Ferguson*)

PILOT:
CAPT. R.I.BONG
CREW C.:
T/SGT. E.E.BARDEN
ASS'T.C.C.:
CPL. W.FINKEL

H-5-LO
42-66847

Sgt Lynd gets his photograph taken alongside the scoreboard of Dick Bong's P-38H-5 42-66847 in late 1943. The 49th FG's ranking ace claimed five kills and one damaged during the Rabaul missions of October-November 1943 (*Steve Ferguson*)

fell to Lt Bleecker, who was flying as No 4, to finish the Ki-61 off, the enemy fighter flying straight into his fire as it slowed at the top of its loop. Just as the Lightning pilot was forced to disengage, the 'Tony' burst into flame and the pilot took to his parachute.

October also got off to a slow start, with only one combat in the first few days. While on patrol in the vicinity of Cape Hopkins, New Britain, Bong surprised a reconnaissance aircraft and slipped in behind it. Four short bursts sent the Ki-46 down in flames, and the enemy pilot probably never knew what hit him.

The 8th FS's Lt James Hagerstrom (a future Korean War F-86 ace) had a much more difficult time getting his Ki-46 three days later, his P-40N struggling to catch the 'Dinah' as it sped along at 18,000 ft over Finschhafen. He had to use war emergency power for a full 12 minutes, flying at an indicated 270 mph and 2700 rpm, before he finally got within firing distance. Later, Hagerstrom related;

'I fired my first burst when his wings filled my sight. It hit him in the left engine, wing root and fuselage. The left engine exploded and the aircraft did a steep wing-over due to the sudden loss of power. The nose, canopy and whole right side of my aircraft was covered with what appeared to be hydraulic fluid. Some seeped into my cockpit, causing a burning and stinging sensation in my eyes. I rolled with the "Dinah", firing again at the left wing root and it caught fire. I rolled over and split-essed, only to find he had hit the water.'

The Allied offensive against the Japanese stronghold of Rabaul was launched on 12 October when large numbers of B-24s and B-25s were despatched to strike the town, and its surrounding airfields. The 9th FS was called on to provide fighter escort, and it was led into action by unit CO, Maj Johnson.

Once they reached the target area, the weather took a turn for the worse, and the P-38s were unable to maintain formation with the bombers. Johnson continued to circle until he saw the B-24s complete their bombing runs and turn for home. It was not until the unit returned to base that the 9th FS realised that senior Lts Ralph Hays, Theron Price and Frank Wunder Jr had all been lost over Lae.

On the 15th all three of the group's squadrons were in action when a large formation of Japanese aircraft were detected heading for Allied positions in New Guinea. The first to be scrambled were the P-40Ns of the 7th FS, closely followed by seven 9th FS P-38s, again led by Maj Johnson. But the fighters of the newly-formed 475th FG beat the latter unit into action, attacking alongside the 7th FS. Capt Carl Aubrey sighted three Vs of 'Val' dive-bombers heading out to sea, and he attacked. Aubrey and Lt Roger Farrell fired on two 'Vals', scoring hits on both of them. The pilots then turned to re-group, but were then attacked by a lone P-38.

While this was going on Lt Bobby Harrison and his wingman chased a 'Hap', but Harrison was interrupted

The 7th FS's Capt Bobby Harrison was squadron operations officer for a time during his tour. He was credited with shooting down a 'Tony' and probably destroying a 'Hamp' whilst serving in New Guinea in 1943 (*Steve Ferguson*)

by a 475th FG Lightning. By this time Johnson and his P-38s were at 22,000 ft in the Oro Bay area, and the unit CO spotted a formation of 18 enemy dive-bombers, accompanied by at least 20 fighters. Johnson reported;

'We dropped our belly tanks and dived to the attack. We headed for a formation of 18 "Vals". The one I attacked started burning and dived straight into the ocean. Lt Swift observed this aeroplane go down in flames. I fired at another "Val" in its dive, and he rolled away smoking heavily. I attacked an "Oscar" that was on the tail of a P-38 at an altitude of about 500 ft. I fired a burst at him and observed the enemy aeroplane hit the water and burn. I attacked two more "Vals" with nil results. I then made a pass at an "Oscar", but with no results. I attacked another "Val" and fired a burst into him. His left wing tank blew up and I saw him crash into the ocean and burn.'

These three victories made Jerry Johnson the 49th's newest ace. The 9th's total score was five 'Vals', four Zekes and two 'Oscars' destroyed.

Just minutes after the 7th FS P-40s had been attacked in error by an unidentified P-38, another near fatal mistake was made when a 9th FS element leader attacked what he thought was a formation of three enemy fighters following a formation of 'Vals'. However, when he closed and opened fire he found that he was attacking P-40s. Once again the 7th was under fire from Lightnings. Two Warhawks were badly damaged, but all returned to base.

Later that afternoon four 8th FS P-40s took off to escort Australian Boomerang fighters that were acting as artillery target spotters over Finschhafen. While the Warhawk pilots circled above the RAAF aircraft, they sighted nine silhouettes high in the sky, and on climbing up to investigate. they found a formation of nine 'Lily' bombers. The P-40 pilots charged into the formation, and despite the fighter escort, they sent five of the bombers down in flames. Capt Joe Littleton and Lt William Runey both scored doubles while Lt James Carter got the fifth.

The 9th FS escorted B-25s to Madang the following day, but only one enemy fighter put in an appearance – it was despatched by Lt George Haniotis. Aircraft from both the 7th and 9th FSs were scrambled on 17 October, the P-38s proceeding to Buna at 28,000 ft, where they

The 9th FS's Lt Jimmie Harris (right), seen here with his crew and their P-38H in 1943, was yet another 49th FG pilot who missed out on being an ace by just one kill. He finished his tour with four confirmed victories and a probable (*Steve Ferguson*)

sighted at least 30 'Oscars' and Zekes in line astern some 7000 ft below them. The P-38s dived to attack and Lt James W Harris knocked the horizontal stabiliser off his first victim, which went spinning straight down. He hit the second from its 'six o'clock' and flames immediately broke out around the engine. Six Zekes fell to the unit that day.

B-24s returned to Rabaul in force on the 23rd, with the 9th FS putting up 16 P-38s, but they initially saw little action. Finally, as they circled at 26,000 ft, the Lightning pilots sighted six to eight enemy fighters in a scattered formation and they went after them. Johnson chased a Zeke which had made a pass at the B-24s. He cut his throttles to keep from overrunning the target and fired from dead astern. There were two explosions and its tail disintegrated. Pieces flew back and bounced off the leading edge of the Lightning's wings as it flew through the wreckage.

This solitary kill took Jerry Johnson's score to seven. Further successes lay ahead for the charismatic 9th FS CO as the campaign in New Guinea reached its climax.

Capt Jerry Johnson sits in the cockpit of his well-weathered P-38H-1 on Kiriwina Island, awaiting the signal to take off. This shot was taken in October 1943 at the height of the aerial assault on Rabaul. The Fifth Air Force waged an intensive bombing campaign against the Japanese stronghold in New Britain in October and November 1943, and the 49th FG was in the thick of the action, escorting medium and heavy bombers. The 9th FS inflicted significant losses on the enemy during these missions, but also suffered heavy attrition to the tune of 16 aircraft destroyed and others damaged – hence the unit's transition onto the P-47 in late November. Johnson claimed six Japanese kills during this period, as well as an Australian Wirraway which he accidentally shot down on 15 November (*John Stanaway*)

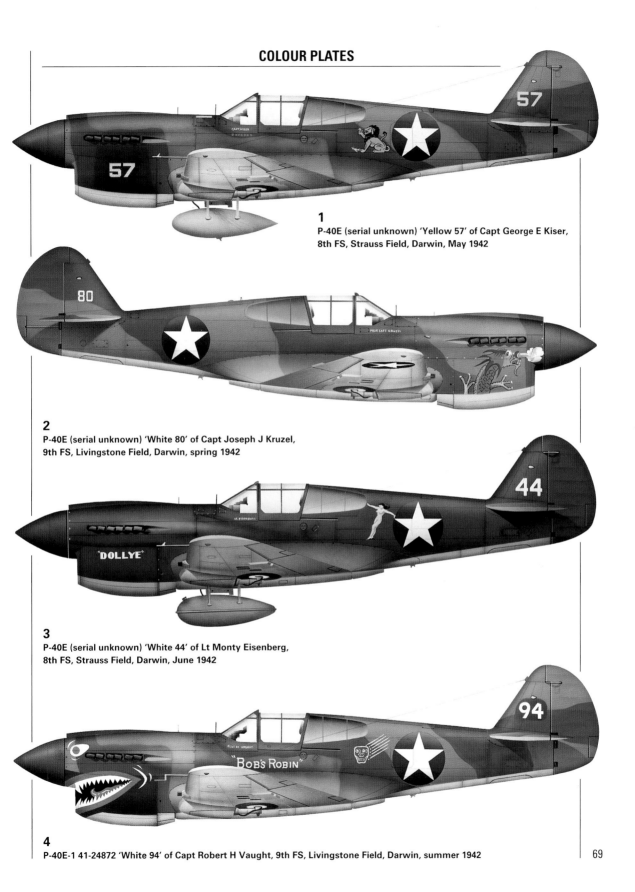

1
P-40E (serial unknown) 'Yellow 57' of Capt George E Kiser,
8th FS, Strauss Field, Darwin, May 1942

2
P-40E (serial unknown) 'White 80' of Capt Joseph J Kruzel,
9th FS, Livingstone Field, Darwin, spring 1942

3
P-40E (serial unknown) 'White 44' of Lt Monty Eisenberg,
8th FS, Strauss Field, Darwin, June 1942

4
P-40E-1 41-24872 'White 94' of Capt Robert H Vaught, 9th FS, Livingstone Field, Darwin, summer 1942

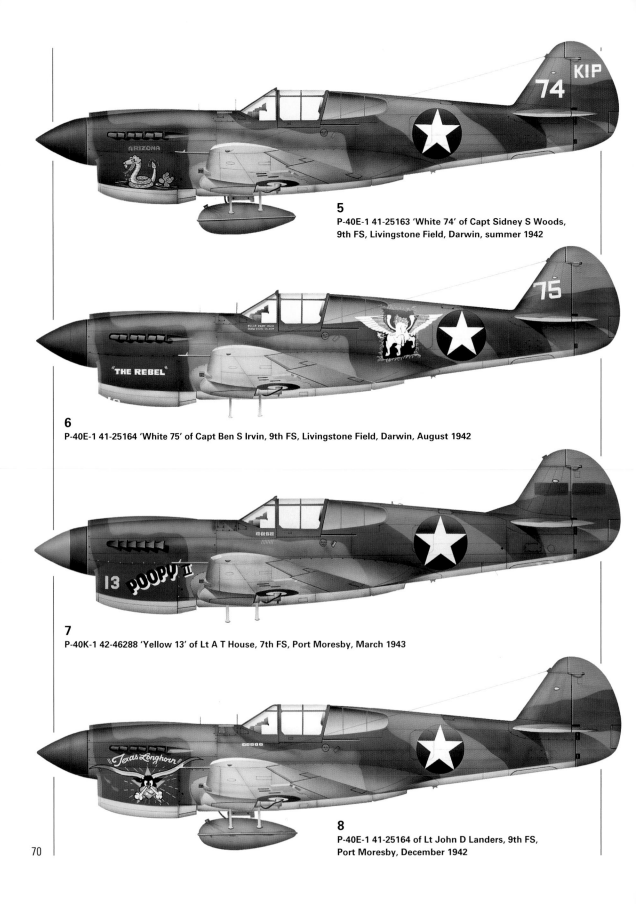

5
P-40E-1 41-25163 'White 74' of Capt Sidney S Woods,
9th FS, Livingstone Field, Darwin, summer 1942

6
P-40E-1 41-25164 'White 75' of Capt Ben S Irvin, 9th FS, Livingstone Field, Darwin, August 1942

7
P-40K-1 42-46288 'Yellow 13' of Lt A T House, 7th FS, Port Moresby, March 1943

8
P-40E-1 41-25164 of Lt John D Landers, 9th FS,
Port Moresby, December 1942

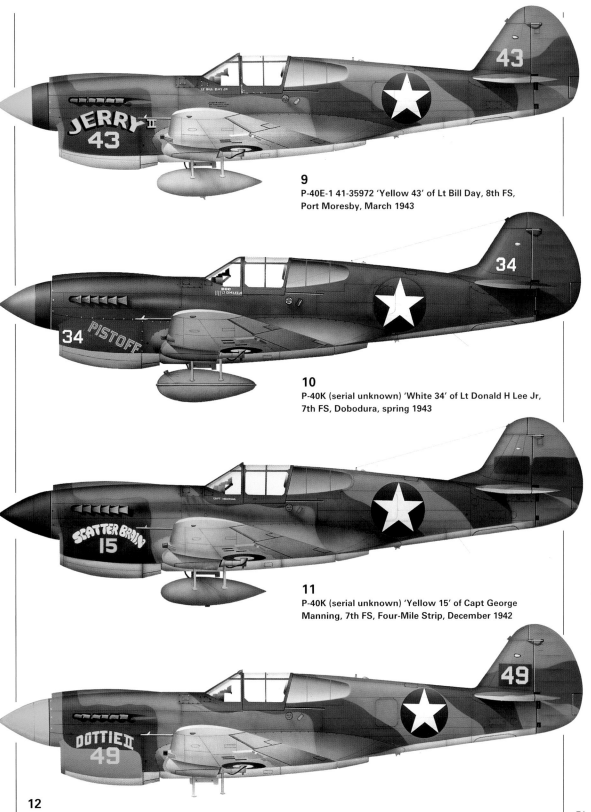

9
P-40E-1 41-35972 'Yellow 43' of Lt Bill Day, 8th FS,
Port Moresby, March 1943

10
P-40K (serial unknown) 'White 34' of Lt Donald H Lee Jr,
7th FS, Dobodura, spring 1943

11
P-40K (serial unknown) 'Yellow 15' of Capt George
Manning, 7th FS, Four-Mile Strip, December 1942

12
P-40E (serial unknown) 'Yellow 49' of Maj Ellis Wright, V Fighter Command HQ, Dobodura, May 1943

13
P-38G-13 43-2208 'White 95' of Capt Bill Haney, 9th FS, Dobodura, October 1943

14
P-38H-1 (serial unknown) 'White 79' of Capt Dick Bong, 9th FS, Dobodura, September 1943

15
P-38G-5 (serial unknown) 'White 73' of Lt Dick Bong, 9th FS, Dobodura, July 1943

16
P-40K (serial unknown) 'White 16' of Lt Clyde V Knisley,
7th FS, Dobodura, July 1943

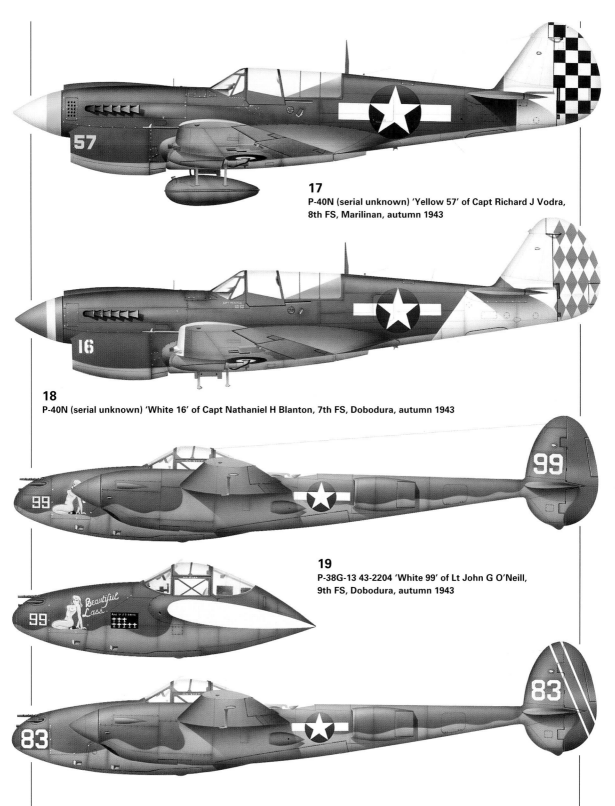

17
P-40N (serial unknown) 'Yellow 57' of Capt Richard J Vodra,
8th FS, Marilinan, autumn 1943

18
P-40N (serial unknown) 'White 16' of Capt Nathaniel H Blanton, 7th FS, Dobodura, autumn 1943

19
P-38G-13 43-2204 'White 99' of Lt John G O'Neill,
9th FS, Dobodura, autumn 1943

20
P-38H-1 (serial unknown) 'White 83' of Capt Gerald Johnson, 9th FS, Dobodura, November 1943

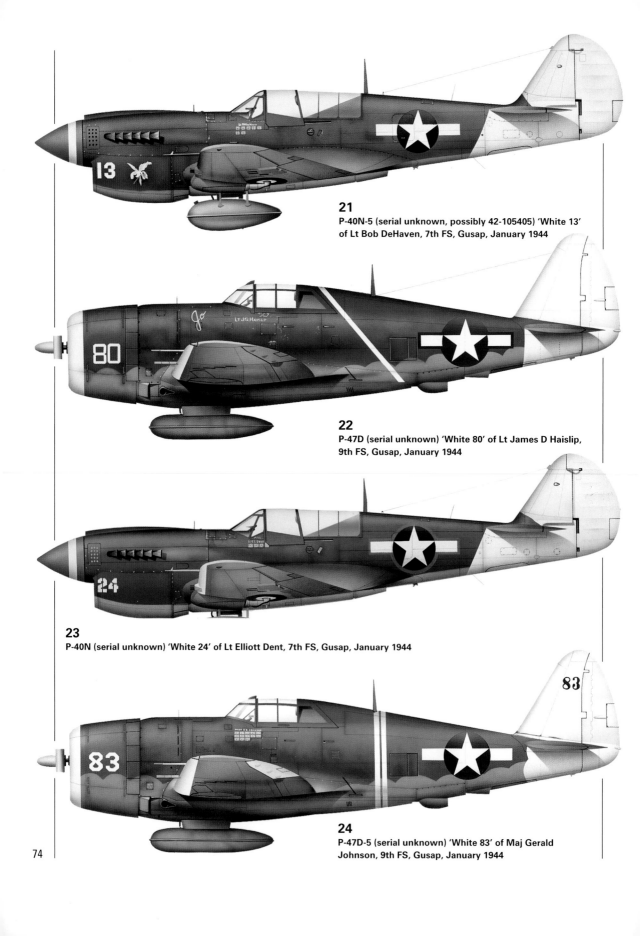

21
P-40N-5 (serial unknown, possibly 42-105405) 'White 13' of Lt Bob DeHaven, 7th FS, Gusap, January 1944

22
P-47D (serial unknown) 'White 80' of Lt James D Haislip, 9th FS, Gusap, January 1944

23
P-40N (serial unknown) 'White 24' of Lt Elliott Dent, 7th FS, Gusap, January 1944

24
P-47D-5 (serial unknown) 'White 83' of Maj Gerald Johnson, 9th FS, Gusap, January 1944

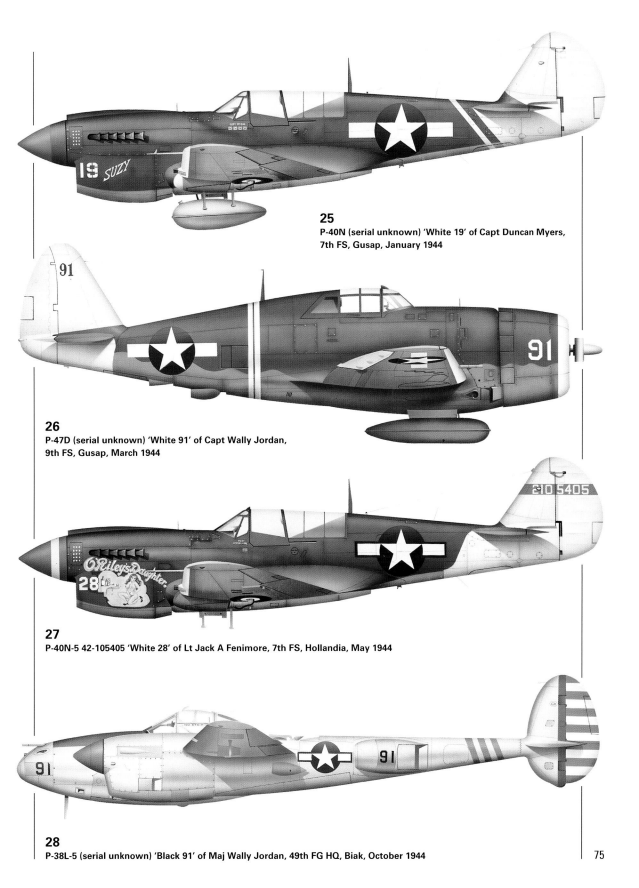

25
P-40N (serial unknown) 'White 19' of Capt Duncan Myers,
7th FS, Gusap, January 1944

26
P-47D (serial unknown) 'White 91' of Capt Wally Jordan,
9th FS, Gusap, March 1944

27
P-40N-5 42-105405 'White 28' of Lt Jack A Fenimore, 7th FS, Hollandia, May 1944

28
P-38L-5 (serial unknown) 'Black 91' of Maj Wally Jordan, 49th FG HQ, Biak, October 1944

29
P-38L-5 (serial unknown) 'Black 83' of Maj Gerald Johnson, 49th FG, Biak, October 1944

30
P-40N-5 42-105826 'Black 7' of Maj Gerald Johnson, 49th FG HQ, Biak, October 1944

31
P-38L-5 (serial unknown) 'Black 13' of Capt Bob DeHaven, 7th FS, Tacloban, November 1944

32
P-38L-1 44-23964 'Yellow 42' of Maj Dick Bong, V Fighter Command, Tacloban, November 1944

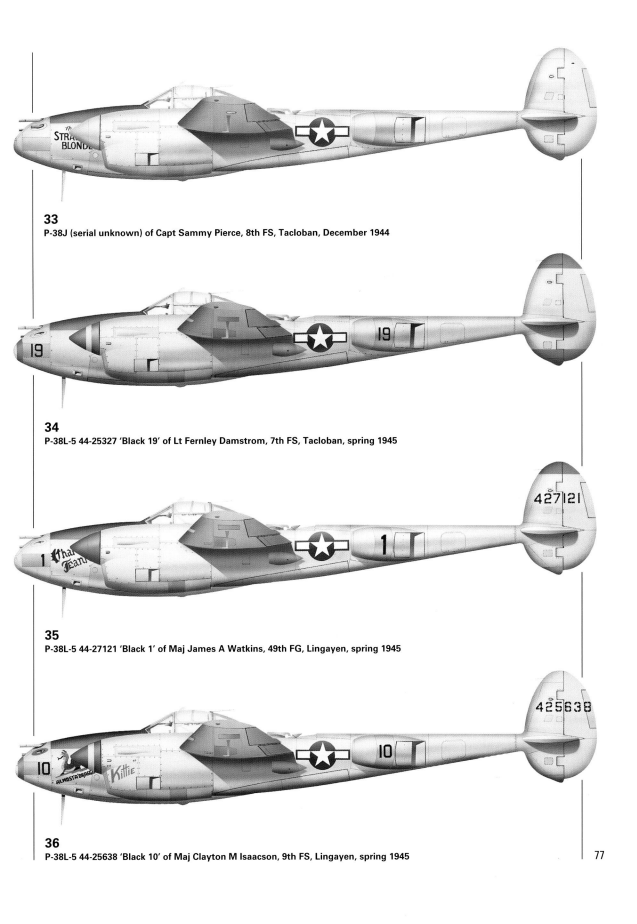

33
P-38J (serial unknown) of Capt Sammy Pierce, 8th FS, Tacloban, December 1944

34
P-38L-5 44-25327 'Black 19' of Lt Fernley Damstrom, 7th FS, Tacloban, spring 1945

35
P-38L-5 44-27121 'Black 1' of Maj James A Watkins, 49th FG, Lingayen, spring 1945

36
P-38L-5 44-25638 'Black 10' of Maj Clayton M Isaacson, 9th FS, Lingayen, spring 1945

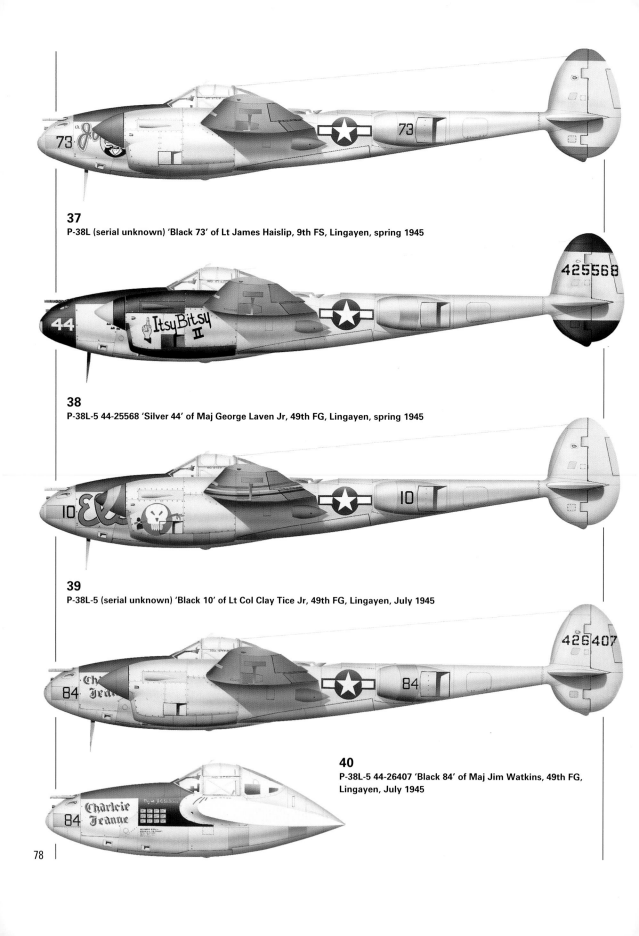

37
P-38L (serial unknown) 'Black 73' of Lt James Haislip, 9th FS, Lingayen, spring 1945

38
P-38L-5 44-25568 'Silver 44' of Maj George Laven Jr, 49th FG, Lingayen, spring 1945

39
P-38L-5 (serial unknown) 'Black 10' of Lt Col Clay Tice Jr, 49th FG, Lingayen, July 1945

40
P-38L-5 44-26407 'Black 84' of Maj Jim Watkins, 49th FG, Lingayen, July 1945

LIGHTNINGS AND THUNDERBOLTS

As Australian infantry units seized the Japanese strongholds of Salamaua and Lae, US aircraft continued to pound the fortress of Rabaul on the northern tip of New Britain. One of the biggest strikes of the campaign took place on 24 Octobet 1943 when the Fifth Air Force assembled its B-25 force for a massive raid. A dozen 9th FS P-38s, led by Dick Bong, were to accompany the medium bombers.

Attacking at low level, the Lightning pilots soon became separated from the bombers when Japanese fighters appeared on the scene. Some six enemy aircraft were shot down, with Lt John O'Neill becoming the day's high scorer – his two Zekes gave him ace status. Bong was having an off day, however, for he fired at three Zekes but failed to score any telling hits. Strafing three luggers provided scant compensation for the loss of his wingman.

Three days later, eight 7th FS P-40s were covering shipping off Finschhafen at 10,000 ft when they spotted nine enemy bombers, escorted by 12 to 15 fighters. Lt Robert DeHaven's flight was sent to take care of the escort. He reported;

'We made our first pass at fighters below me at 2000 to 3000 ft. I fired a three-second burst at a Zeke but saw no destructive results. He rolled onto his back as I passed over him, pulling up to the right to meet any fighters coming down on us. As I looked back I saw the Zeke Lt Myers was firing at burning in the trees. I climbed rapidly to 1000 ft and saw another Zeke circling the ship Lt Myers had shot down. I went down for another pass, and I observed two more fires from crashed aeroplanes – one of which I believe Lt Germain shot down.

'The Zeke pilot apparently did not observe my approach, as he circled slowly to the left. I dropped down behind him, expended approximately a four-second burst and he rolled on his back and dove into the trees a short

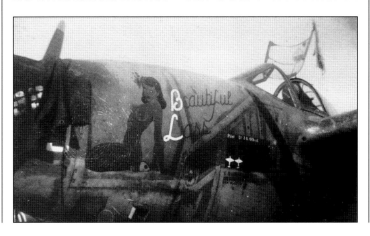

Eight-kill ace 1Lt John G 'Jump' O'Neill flew P-38G-13 43-2204 *Beautiful Lass* **from mid-1943 until he transferred out of the group in November of that same year** (*Steve Ferguson*)

distance from the burning aeroplanes. He neither burned nor exploded when he crashed. I pulled up again to watch Zekes above me, before turning for home.

'As I looked down the coast I observed a P-40 and a "Tony" circling and making head-on passes. I immediately proceeded to join the fight. As I approached the "Tony" from the left, he was turning toward the right, and evidently observed me coming as he straightened out, climbing slightly. I banked sharply and closed in on his tail. I fired until I was forced to break off, coming close to ramming him. As I looked back, he was hanging on his back with his prop barely turning over. He immediately went into a vertical dive and the pilot bailed out at approximately 1500 ft. As he bailed out, the other P-40 made another pass. The "Tony" exploded when it crashed.'

The 7th FS was credited with seven kills overall, Capt John Brenner getting two 'Hamps' and Lt David Germain a 'Hamp' and a 'Lily'.

BONG SCORES OVER RABAUL

The 9th FS performed yet another bomber escort mission to Rabaul on 29 October, during which its pilots chalked up another seven victories. Bong led once again, and this time his aim was far better than it had been five days earlier. Arriving over the target area at 20,000 ft, the ranking 49th FG ace sighted enemy fighters forming up to attack a formation of B-24s. Bong ordered his pilots to drop their belly tanks and follow him down as he power dived towards the Japanese aircraft. In his usual laconic style, he later reported;

'Zekes attacked from directly above and I made a pass on one below me after it had gone through the bombers. Two Zekes jumped on my tail and I was driven down to 3000 ft with my wingman. I fired two shots at Zekes on the way down, but with no results. I made a head-on attack at one Zeke at 1000 ft and he crashed out of control. I chased two more Zekes toward Open Bay and shot one down in flames and damaged the other one. I broke off the engagement due to a lack of ammunition.'

Like Bong, Lt John G O'Neill also claimed two kills, taking his tally to eight – he was posted home the following month, tour-expired. Lt Charles L Ralph downed a 'Hamp' and Lt Raymond A Swift a Zeke during the same engagement. The unit's only casualty in return was second element pilot Lt John Stowe, whose fighter was shot up by a lone Zeke as he turned for home. Four 20 mm and twenty 7 mm 'slugs' hit the right nacelle of Stowe's P-38, damaging the aircraft but not wounding the pilot. He managed to limp home.

The 9th FS's P-38s had seen heavy usage since the summer, and they were now proving difficult to keep airworthy. With no replacements in sight, it was becoming a major task for the groundcrews to put a dozen Lightnings into the air at any one time. The pilots were well aware that something had to change, and they would soon find out what.

Returning to Rabaul on 2 November as fighter cover for low-flying B-25s sent to attack shipping in Simpson Harbour, the unit was led on this occasion by squadron CO Capt Jerry Johnson. Heavy flak greeted the USAAF aircraft and enemy fighters soon put in an appearance too. As the Lightnings and Mitchells roared across the harbour bombing and strafing enemy vessels, Capt Johnson encountered five enemy fighters. A 45-

Also featured in the previous chapter, P-38F-5 42-12655 *"Sooner"* was the first Lightning assigned to Capt Jerry Johnson upon his arrival in New Guinea. It is seen here with Johnson's crew chief, Sgt Harlerode. Note the unfinished nose number ('80'), which had only recently been applied when this photograph was taken (*Steve Ferguson*)

degree deflection shot into a Zeke set its belly tank on fire, and pieces flew off the aircraft as it rolled over and crashed in flames. A second Zeke, downed west of Simpson Harbour, added another 'flamer' to Johnson's bag. Another to taste success on this day was 9th FS veteran Capt William Haney, who reported;

'We dropped our belly tanks and climbed to the attack. I observed Capt Johnson fire on a Zeke and set it smoking. I fired at a second and made some hits on him. We proceeded around the harbour above the town. As we went south towards the mouth of the Warango River, we engaged about 20 Zekes and "Oscars". I made a pass at one Zeke climbing and opened fire at 45 degrees, 100 yards range. I exploded his engine and I saw large chunks of his engine blown off. This Zeke started smoking as he was going down. I opened fire on three Zekes that were in string formation and made a head-on pass at them.

'The lead Zeke turned when he was about 200 ft away, and I saw bullets shear plates from under the engine, centre section of the wing and towards the tail of the fuselage. The Zeke seemed to jump in the air as it stalled and started down. I fired at an "Oscar" while I was climbing vertically. I made hits on this "Oscar". I made two more passes on Zekes with unknown results.'

Unfortunately for Haney there were no witnesses, and his two Zekes were listed as probables. But Lts Douglas Barrett, Norman Hyland, Stanley Johnson and Alfred Lewelling were all credited with single kills. There were two casualties – Lt Francis Love was killed and Lt Carl Planck collided with a Zeke, although he managed to retain sufficient control to ditch his P-38 off the east coast of New Britain. Through the assistance of natives and Australian coast watchers, he finally returned to Nadzab.

By 5 November, when the 9th FS was next over Rabaul, enemy fighter forces had been greatly depleted by the massive bombing attacks of the past few weeks. Bong led 11 Lightnings on another B-24 escort mission and, flying at 20,000 ft, the P-38s sighted 15 enemy fighters heading from the northwest. Dick Bong's mission report read in part;

'I came down on two from the rear and fired a short burst into the last one from about 100 yards and he blew up. I fired a long burst at another and he split-essed, but never pulled out. He blew up about 5000 ft above the ground. Broke off combat for lack of gas and ammunition.'

This combat produced his 20th and 21st victories (both Zekes), putting his total close to the 26 scored by the ranking US ace of World War 1, Eddie Rickenbacker. Gen Kenney assured Bong that he would have every opportunity to reach, and even surpass, that mark.

Two days later Capt John O'Neill led seven P-38s to Rabaul. Although enemy fighters were sighted, there were no confirmed victories, and the mission ended in tragedy when Lt Stanley Johnson – Bong's favourite wingman – chased a fighter inland from the harbour. He never returned. Bong refused to fly for a few days, but on 14 November he and Lt Ralph Wandrey took off on a special mission to Rabaul. They found no enemy aircraft.

THE 9th FS RE-EQUIP

On 12 November Jerry Johnson made the announcement that the 9th FS had been expecting, and dreading – the unit would be re-equipping with the Republic P-47 Thunderbolt instead of receiving replacement P-38s. Other changes included a move for the 49th FG from Dobodura to Gusap, and a change of nickname for the 8th FS. Lt Dick Vodra asked a friend in the Walt Disney Studios to supply a squadron insignia, and the resulting drawing of a black lamb dressed in flying gear prompted the unit to change its nickname from the 'Eightballs' to the 'Blacksheep'.

Following the 8th FS's move from Dobodura, the squadron was predominantly involved in supporting the Australian Army's 7th Division

1Lt Richard J Vodra of the 8th FS decorated the rudder of his P-40N 'Yellow 41' with black checks in the autumn of 1943 at Marilinan. Vodra was responsible for obtaining a Disney cartoon of a 'black sheep' which became the 8th FS mascot, and gave the squadron its nickname (*Steve Ferguson*)

in its offensive against the Japanese who, in return, had started striking the unit's new base at Gusap. Capt Clyde 'Smiley' Barnett, a Darwin veteran who had been grounded for a time, decided it was time the 'Blacksheep' retaliated. Two missions were therefore flown on 7 November, with the morning strike being led by Barnett, with Flt Off Walt Linder as his wingman, and Lt Jim Carter, with Lt Nelson Flack on his wing.

Approaching Alexishafen at a height of 10,000 ft, the P-40 pilots sighted at least 25 Zekes and dived on the attack. Closing to point blank range, Barnett, Linder and Flack opened fire and three Japanese fighters burst into flames. Barnett, Linder and Carter then broke away and headed home, leaving Flack with plenty of targets. After some wild manoeuvring, he managed to down his second victim, before he too dived to safety.

That afternoon the 8th, now led by CO Capt Ernest Harris, returned to the area with eight P-40s. The first group of enemy fighters that was spotted escaped in the haze, but six encountered near Bogadjim stayed to fight it out. Lt Charles Peterson raked one from stem to stern before he was forced to dodge another, and Lt Philip Hurst shot one down, which was seen to crash in the trees. Lt Joel Thorvaldson, who was flying wingman to Capt Robert White, reported;

'I followed Capt White as he chased a Zeke which was at the top of a loop. I observed White's fire hitting from 90 degrees deflection. The Zeke

Lt Philip Hurst of the 8th FS and his attractive P-40N *ANA MAY*. Hurst scored his solitary combat victory on 7 November 1943 (*Steve Ferguson*)

dropped off one wing towards me, and I observed my tracers hitting him along the fuselage. I popped my stick to avoid hitting him and saw his wing fall off. I then pulled up. I dived on another Zeke, which was trailing a P-40. The Zeke turned towards me and I fired head-on at him until I was forced to break away. This Zeke rolled over on its back as he passed me at an altitude of 1500 ft and crashed into the trees upside down.'

On 15 November the Japanese launched a heavy bombing raid on the Gusap complex, which was now home to both the 3rd Attack Squadron's A-20s and elements of the 49th FG. The 8th FS had been expecting such an attack, and had maintained standing patrols over the base – this proved to be a wise tactical move. Lt Bernie Makowski was leading eight fighters when his patrol sighted 24 bombers, escorted by 30 fighters, heading for their base. One of the first to attack was element leader Lt Robert Aschenbrener, who, along with his wingman, flew straight into the middle of the Japanese force. He coolly chandelled out to the edge of the enemy formation and latched onto the tail of an 'Oscar', having evaded two Zekes in the process.

It took Aschenbrener just two bursts to set his opponent on fire. Convinced that the Ki-43 was doomed, he broke away and set off after three Zekes, the P-40 pilot firing at one all the way through a turn. He scored hits all over the cockpit.

Despite claiming six fighters destroyed, the 8th FS only managed to down one 'Lily' bomber, which fell to Lt Donald Meuten. Taking it apart piece by piece, his fire initially removed the forward canopy, then he gutted the cockpit and finally he cut off part of the right engine.

As November 1943 ended, it was time for more combat veterans to go home. Maj Ray Melikian of the 7th FS was succeeded by Capt Arland Stanton as unit CO, while Capt Bernie Makowski took over as 8th FS boss from double ace Maj Ernest Harris. In a further move, Maj Jerry Johnson led the 8th FS's newly arrived P-47 Thunderbolts to Gusap on 10 December. It had been a timely move, for Japanese 'Tony' fighters had streaked in to strafe the base at low level. They were met by anti-aircraft fire, but there was also a surprise in store for the raiders as they were leaving. Johnson explained;

'At 0900 hrs, about 20 miles north of Gusap strip, while our flight was at 9000 ft, we observed eight enemy fighters. They were in a scattered

A shirtless Maj Gerald Johnson sits in the cockpit of his P-47D Thunderbolt at Gusap in late 1943. Although not a fan of the big Republic fighter, he nevertheless scored two kills while flying it (*John Stanaway*)

Jerry Johnson primarily flew this particular P-47D (serial unknown) until he was posted home to attend command school on 29 January 1944. Marked up with CO stripes stripes, it is seen here at Gusap whilst in the process of having Johnson's victory tally applied. Note the Vultee Vengeance parked behind the Thunderbolt (*John Stanaway*)

formation at about 5000 ft. When first observed, they were coming from the southeast of the valley. We dived to attack. Our speed was so great on the initial attack that we only broke up their flight. We made repeated attacks, mostly head-on or front quarter. I hit one "Tony" in the engine and it started burning. The pilot bailed out and an Australian patrol shot him on the ground. I saw an aeroplane burning on the ground. This was probably one of the "Tonys" shot down by Capt Markey. The "Tony" I shot down went straight in and crashed in the trees.'

That same day the 7th FS sent two flights on a fighter sweep to Hansa Bay, the first being led by Lt Bobby Harrison, with CO Capt Arland Stanton on his wing. The other element comprised Capt Sheldon Brinson and Lt Bob DeHaven. At approximately 0920 hrs, Harrison called out 15 to 20 Zekes, 'Tonys' and 'Oscars' and attacked immediately. Stanton shot down an 'Oscar' at once. DeHaven reported;

'We dived slightly to pick up speed, and I prepared to turn into two "Tonys" that were closing on my tail. Suddenly, two closed on our left side, and I thought the second was making a pass on Capt Brinson. Rolling slightly, I expended a one- or two-second burst and pulled up over him to observe the results. Capt Brinson said that although no damage was visible, the pilot bailed out and the aircraft crashed near Alexishafen.

'Just as I pulled up, the "Tony" behind me shot away my rudder control. As I started down, a Zeke pulled through my sights and I gave it a snap shot with no results. With no rudder control, I was forced to aileron roll straight down until my speed was well over 400 mph. As I neared the ground, the "Tony" was still on my tail, shooting out my hydraulic system, radio, left guns, etc. I straightened out and headed for a low cloud seen against the foothills. Suddenly, the "Tony" broke off in a right chandelle and departed.'

Now an ace, Bob DeHaven headed for Gusap. With no flaps or landing gear, and no communications, he attempted a belly landing beside the strip. Using his ailerons, he lined himself up neatly, only to have a C-47 suddenly appear before him with gear and flaps down, coming in to land. DeHaven thrust the throttle forward, dropped his left wing and managed to scrape past the transport. Now back at about 100 ft, the P-40 pilot managed to make a broad, flat turn and came in for a successful belly landing.

But there was to be little rest for DeHaven. Two days later he was flying one of eight P-40Ns put up by the 7th FS to patrol over their base. Circling at 10,000 ft, the Warhawk pilots spotted nine 'Betty' bombers and fifteen escorting fighters in loose formation.

Element leader Lt Lou Martin managed to put enough 'slugs' into one of the bombers to send it down trailing smoke before his radiator was hit, sending him out of the fight. Capt Sheldon Brinson also went after a 'Betty', but he received a telling blast from its tail gunner. Badly wounded and briefly knocked out, Brinson recovered enough to make it back to Gusap. However, blurred vision and worsening wounds prevented him from making a safe landing, and his fighter overran the runway and ploughed through the scrub for about 100 yards before it came to a halt. Brinson was pulled from the wreckage and flown to hospital, where he eventually recovered to be repatriated.

Meanwhile, Lt DeHaven was thwarted in his attempts to attack the bombers and turned his attentions to the escorting 'Oscars'. Stalking two Ki-43s, he was almost within gun range when a pair of P-47s arrived above the 'Oscars' and they split up. One went into a right turn, which gave DeHaven his chance of getting in a good burst – the fighter rolled over and crashed in flames.

GROUND ATTACK

There was to be no further aerial successes for the 49th FG during the rest of December, pilots instead concentrating on flying bomber escort missions and conducting bombing and strafing missions of their own. The use of napalm by fighters in-theatre had just begun, and the Thunderbolt pilots of the 9th FS were beginning to see just how destructive eight 0.50-cal machine guns could be against ground targets.

On 2 January 1944 US ground forces landed at Saidor, 100 miles north of Finschhafen on the northeastern New Guinea coast. A-20s bombed and strafed the beach prior to the troops coming ashore, with 7th FS P-40Ns providing top cover for the bombers. The Warhawk pilots later

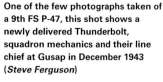

One of the few photographs taken of a 9th FS P-47, this shot shows a newly delivered Thunderbolt, squadron mechanics and their line chief at Gusap in December 1943 (*Steve Ferguson*)

headed inland to prevent Japanese aircraft from Wewak attacking the beachhead. Soon spotting nine 'Lily' bombers and 34 fighters heading for Saidor, Lt Duncan Myers led his flight in an attack on the escorts and sent an 'Oscar' down in flames, while his wingman, Lt George Allen, got a Zeke.

Bob DeHaven fired at several 'Tonys' but saw no results, and then sighted a P-40 and a Ki-61 circling in combat and decided to join in. He later reported;

'I immediately dived down, getting a two-second deflection shot with no results. As I pulled out, the other P-40 made another pass, but still no results. I then pulled back into the merry-go-round, and blanking him out, fired a long three- or four-second burst. As he flew through my sights the right wing broke off about two feet from the fuselage and the aeroplane spun down, the pilot bailing out.'

DeHaven also noted;

'It is my opinion that the P40N-5 can definitely out-climb, out-zoom and out-turn the "Tony" at all altitudes and speeds.'

Once the fighters had been dispersed, Lt Myers and Maj Selmon Wells tore into the 'Lilys', and each shot one of them down.

The Japanese struck Gusap on 15 January when Tony fighters made a surprise low-level attack, destroying one A-20 and two P-47s. Damage to other facilities was limited, however. Three days later the 9th FS retaliated when Maj Jerry Johnson led his P-47s against Wewak, joining the 7th and 8th FS who were escorting B-24s to the same target. There was only one air combat reported on this date – Maj Johnson downed a Zeke.

Concerned at intelligence reports of a continued build-up of Japanese aircraft at the four air bases in the Wewak area, Gen Kenney ordered a Fifth Air Force-wide attack on 23 January. Warhawks and Thunderbolts

Lt Howard Oglesby of the 9th FS christened his P-47D *Bigasburd*, which aptly summed up most pilots' feelings towards the Thunderbolt at Gusap. They found the aircraft heavy and unresponsive in comparison with the P-38. Oglesby scored four victories after the unit re-equipped with Lightning (*Steve Ferguson*)

of the 49th FG were all airborne escorting medium and heavy bombers. Capt Arland Stanton led his 17 P-40s on the right flank of the B-24s, following them until they dropped their bombs and turned for home. He then led his charges into combat with defending Japanese fighters.

Lt John Haher swept his flight through a gaggle of 'Oscars' and shot two of them down. His wingman, Lt Jay Rogers, damaged another before they continued their escort duty. In Stanton's flight, only element leader Lt Elliott Dent scored. His first victim exploded after a head-on attack, and he then downed Zeke number two with a neat deflection shot.

DeHaven's flight was attacked by Ki-43s, and Lt Marion Hawke intervened in a combat in which Lt Jack Suggs' aircraft was badly damaged. But DeHaven was unable to help Lt John Crowley, whom he spotted just above the water with a Ki-43 on his tail. A burst of fire from the enemy sent the P-40 rolling into the sea. Moments later DeHaven exacted revenge by swooping down on the low-flying 'Oscar' and firing at it from point blank range. With its cockpit and fuselage in flames, the fighter also crashed into the sea.

This escort mission would prove to be the most successful sortie of the war for 8th FS pilot Lt James Hagerstrom. Having been grounded for a time with malaria, he had been declared fit enough to fly on the maximum effort mission of the 23rd. On his return, Hagerstrom reported;

'Our squadron of 16 P-40s in four flights took off at 0945 hrs. I was flight leader of "Blue Flight". We proceeded to Boram, flying at 20,000 ft. Over Boram at 1130 hrs, I observed 10 to 15 Zeros ("Hamps") coming down from above. We dropped our belly tanks and dove on four to five Zeros chasing four P-38s down to about 10,000 ft. My wingman and I were flying alone. I made a high tail-on pass at a "Hamp" at 10,000 ft. I fired a good burst into him at 100 yards, closing to 50 yards. My wingman observed him going down in flames.

'We dived again and I made a pass at the last "Hamp" flight at 5000 ft. I got a burst in at one of the fighters, and had just pulled up in a turn to observe my shots when a second "Hamp" latched onto me. A third

machine pulled over onto the tail of my wingman, Lt Bodak, who in turn pulled up and shot the "Hamp" off my tail while his "Hamp" was still firing at him. I observed the one that Lt Bodak shot at drop into the water. I pulled around and shot the "Hamp" off Bodak's tail, and he observed him strike the water.

'Two Hamp came down from above and I pulled up, giving them a burst. One turned into me and made a head-on pass. I put a good burst into his engine and belly, passing close enough to feel his prop wash. I put another burst into the second "Hamp", and he also made a deliberate close head-on pass. I saw tracers going into his cowling. The next pass we made was at 2000 ft when I attacked a lone "Hamp". I put a long burst into him from close astern and watched my blue nose bursting along his wings and fuselage. He then burst into flames and fell into the sea, observed by Lt Bodak. He went after a "Hamp" that was chasing two P-38s. I saw this one crash into the sea and the pilot bail out.

'Two or three more came out of the clouds from above us, and I saw a "Tony" pulling onto the tails of two P-38s. We pulled around and followed him up. The P-38s started a Lufbery and we pulled up on the "Tony's" tail. I gave him a short burst from short range and saw hits. He did a steep wingover and I followed, turning with him. He levelled out and I gave him a long burst from short range. He started smoking, then caught fire, rolled over and went in from 1500 ft. Lt Bodak, flying close behind me, saw him hit the water. We made passes on two or three more single "Hamps" and made some good hits, damaging them. I was then out of ammo so we went home.'

Hagerstrom, who was now an ace, was credited with three 'Hamps' and a 'Tony', and Bodak with two 'Hamps'. 'White Flight' also got in the fight, and its leader, Lt Louis Graton, downed a Zeke, as did Lt George Smerchek.

Lt James Hagerstrom of the 8th FS became an ace during a classic dogfight on 23 January 1944 over Wewak, New Guinea, when he downed four enemy aircraft to take his score to six. A few years later he would claim another 8.5 victories over MiG-15s while flying F-86F Sabres during the Korean War with the 67th FBS/18th FBG. Hagerstrom was one of seven American fighter pilots to achieve ace status in two wars (*Steve Ferguson*)

MORE COMMAND CHANGES

There was no further scoring for the 49th FG for the rest of the month, but there were a number of significant command changes, particularly the departure of group CO Lt Col Jim Selman and his replacement by a veteran of the Pacific air war, Lt Col David Campbell. Maj Jerry Johnson was also sent back home to command school, and he was succeeded as 9th FS CO by his deputy, Capt Wally Jordan. Finally, Capt Bernie Makowski, who had only been the 8th FS CO for a short time, was transferred to V Fighter Command staff and his place taken at the head of the unit by Maj Bob McHale.

February's first action came on the 3rd when the 7th FS were escorting A-20s sent to attack Dagua airfield. A flight of P-40s caught three 'Oscars' taking off, but only Lt Roger Farrell was able to overtake one of the Ki-43s and send it crashing into the sea. Three days later the 7th FS strafed Muschu Island, where its pilots found a mixed force of Japanese fighters. Stanton was providing top cover at 8000 ft when the enemy appeared, and he immediately dived and shot a Zeke down into the sea. This kill gave the 7th FS CO ace status.

Three more 8th FS P-40Ns were sweeping over the island at just 400 ft when more enemy fighters were reported. Reversing their course, Lts Elfred Elofson, Marion Felts and Donald Meuten quickly shot three more enemy aircraft down into the water.

Maj McHale and his squadron, along with four pilots from the 7th FS, returned to Muschu Island on the 14th, and on this occasion Lt Elofson's flight was the first to see action. Two Zekes were sighted over Dillman Harbour at 4000 ft, and Lt Donald Meuten caught the trailing one and swiftly despatched it.

Crossing Cape Moem, the 8th FS dropped to 2000 ft and sighted several flights of enemy aircraft. They turned to attack, and at the same time the four 7th FS pilots flying top cover at 8000 ft dived down to join the fray. As the Japanese fighters turned to meet the 8th FS, a flight of four 'Oscars' was attacked by the four P-40s from above. Before they knew

Maj Gerald Johnson (left) and Capt Wally Jordan at Gusap in January 1944. Johnson and Jordan had both flown P-39s with the 54th FG in the Aleutians prior to being posted to the 49th FG in April 1943. Firm friends, they served together in the 9th FS, Jordan replacing Johnson as CO of the unit in late January 1944. This photograph was taken at Gusap just prior to Johnson handing command of the unit over to Jordan. Johnson had by then become a top ace, and he would later lead the Group. He was killed on 7 October 1945 when the B-25 transport that he was flying entered a severe storm over Japan and crashed. Johnson had the option of bailing out of the aircraft, but instead gave his parachute to a passenger aboard the 49th FG transport and then attempted a crash landing, which was unsuccessful (*Steve Ferguson*)

what was happening, all four had been sent down in flames by Lts Robert Croft, Fenton Epling, Roger Farrell and James Keck.

With the 8th FS formation now separated, the aerial engagement broke up into a series of individual dogfights. Lt David Winternitz got an 'Oscar' with his second volley, but new pilot Lt Ed Glascock found himself alone and under attack from a 'Tony'. With his Warhawk badly damaged, he only managed to escape thanks to the timely intervention of 1Lt Nelson Flack, who shot the Ki-61 down. Glascock managed to limp home, but Flack was forced to belly land his P-40 in swamp land when it ran out of fuel some 60 miles from home. Australian commando Sgt Hector Henstridge was parachuted in to help Flack make the difficult and dangerous journey home.

Maj McHale led his squadron back to Wewak on the morning of the 15th, where they engaged in a swirling dogfight with several 'Tonys' and 'Oscars'. Lt Bob Aschenbrener led his flight in first in an attempt to break up a formation of 'Oscars', before doing the same to the 'Tonys'. Aschenbrener and McHale each downed single 'Tonys', while Lt John Porteous got a 'Hamp' and a 'Zeke', despite his fighter's engine being down on power. Other scorers were Lts Averette Lee, Harold Sawyer and James Reynolds.

ACTION OVER WEWAK

The Japanese continued to build up their ground forces in the Wewak area for the rest of the month, and Fifth Air Force heavy bombers pounded them for four days in a row. These raids did not provoke much aerial resistance, however, although 7th FS CO Stanton did manage to pick off a single 'Oscar'.

It was around this time that Capt Dick Bong returned from 60 days leave, but not to the 49th FG. He was now a V Fighter Command Headquarters pilot, which meant that he was free to roam the area at will looking for Japanese aircraft to shoot down. On 8 March, flying with fellow 'freelancing' ace Maj Tom Lynch, he found three 'Oscars' near Dagua airstrip. Lynch shot down one but Bong missed his. He chased another Ki-43 all the way to the coast, where he caught him in a turn, but as Lynch was flying above a cloud layer at the time there was no witness to Bong's kill.

Stanton and his 7th FS met a formation of 'Oscars' over Wewak on the 12th while escorting A-20s over Borum village. Stanton, together with Lts William Ferris, James O' Neill, Lemuel Pollock and Jack Suggs, were all successful. Three of the enemy fell in flames and two splashed into the sea. As the fleeing 'Oscars' sought refuge, they were intercepted by the 8th FS. A wild dogfight ensued, and a further nine Ki-43s were claimed by the 49th FG.

The man who did most of the damage was Lt Donald Meuten, who scored his last victories in this combat to 'make ace' – he was posted Missing In Action after the engine of his P-40N-5 42-105834 failed on 7 May 1944 . He reported;

'There were 20 fighters – "Oscars" and Zekes – seen during the course of combat. After dropping our belly tanks, our flight delayed until we saw an opening. The first element went after two above and I led mine into two that were turning into us from beneath. After following an "Oscar" from 360 degrees, I got a 45-degree shot at about 100 ft. He immediately burst into flames, rolled over on his back and went down. I then pulled up straight and did a vertical roll and saw a silver "Oscar" in a turn. I did an Immelman and got a short shot at him. He started a 360-degree turn, I skidded up fast, did an aileron roll and got a 45-degree shot at about 200 ft. He immediately exploded, did a snap roll and, burning fiercely, fell into the water.

'I then pulled up and looked for some more at this time. I observed a green "Oscar" pulling up straight and took a short burst at him and got a piece of cowling off him, but it did him virtually no damage, as afterwards I saw him do an Immelman and someone else shot him down in flames – I do not know who. I then saw a Zeke out-turn two other P-40s, giving me a perfect 90-degree shot. I closed to 45 degrees, firing a long burst and getting within 300 ft of him. His cockpit blew up and the canopy came off. Orange flame enveloped the entire fuselage.'

Other victors were McHale, Capt Elofson and Lts Felts, Burton, Hall, Lee and Robert Sweeney.

The 9th FS started scoring again on 13 March when Capt Ralph Wandrey caught an 'Oscar' over Wewak. Also airborne that day was the group CO, together with staffer Capt Bob McDaris, who flew with the 7th FS on an escort mission. After the 9th FS broke up the 'Oscar' formation, the Ki-43s were picked off by the P-40Ns. As they hugged the hilltops, the 7th FS pilots dropped down to make short work of a trio of 'Oscars'. Campbell and McDaris both scored, as did future ace Lt Joel Paris of the 7th.

Jordan led the 9th on another escort mission the next day, the P-47s going to Boron. He sighted half a dozen Ki-43s in the target area and dived on them. Jordan later reported;

'I made a head-on pass, climbing with the "Oscar" who was beginning a diving turn into me. He steepened his dive, passing directly in front of

Capt Wilbert Arthur saw considerable action with the 9th FS from the autumn of 1943 until he was shot down over Formosa in April 1945 – he became the only member of the 49th FG to become a prisoner of war. Arthur wrote off a P-47 in a heavy landing during the 9th FS's brief time with the Thunderbolt (*Steve Ferguson*)

me. I pushed over slowly, firing at the same time. From straight and level, I ended up in a 70-degree dive. I observed my blue nose exploding about the cockpit and engine, and Lt Howes, my wingman, observed this "Oscar" going down, burning fiercely. The combat lasted five to ten minutes, and at no time was the flight broken up badly. Twice, enemy aircraft were forced to break away on tail passes because of the flight's proper use of the two-ship element.'

Lt Edward Howes was also credited with an Oscar.

When the P-47s went to Wewak on the 15th, lead by Capt Wandrey, only three enemy aircraft were encountered in the air. Lt Bill Huisman made a head-on pass at a 'Tony' that almost ended in a collision. He managed to get onto its tail and shoot it down – it would be the 9th FS's last P-47 victory.

Meanwhile, Bob DeHaven led the 7th FS on an escort mission for A-20s raiding Kairiru Islands. As the bombers turned for home, they were attacked by a number of 'Oscars'. DeHaven caught one making a head-on pass on a bomber and then turned onto the tail of another, firing all the way. As DeHaven flew by the Ki-43, it rolled onto its back and plunged into the sea. It was DeHaven's ninth victory, and the 7th FS's last kill of the Wewak campaign.

There was, however, one more victory to be scored by the 8th FS. On 11 April the unit was flying what was now regarded as a 'milk run' – escorting A-20s to an abandoned airfield in the Wewak area. As they flew over the target at 10,000 ft, a lone 'Tony' was spotted above them. Lt Bob Aschenbrener began to climb after it, but rather than flee, the Japanese pilot dived for the shoreline. As the five P-40Ns closed, the Japanese pilot turned and attacked. Return fire came immediately, and finally a long burst from Lt Ed Glascock downed the enemy.

On returning to base, the pilots could not help but wonder about the strange encounter with the solitary Ki-61.

Lt James Haislip spent much of his tour with the 9th FS flying this P-47D, although the squadron re-equipped with P-38Js before he left and he shot down a 'Val' dive-bomber with the latter type (*Author*)

ISLAND HOPPING

With eastern New Guinea and New Britain now secure, Allied forces turned their attentions to the west. Gen Douglas MacArthur put 52,000 men ashore in Dutch New Guinea in April 1944, and they soon seized Hollandia on the northern coast. Tadji fell soon afterwards.

With the airfield at Hollandia captured intact, the 49th FG received orders to move in as soon as possible in order to cover bombing raids now being mounted on Biak, still further to the west. The latter boasted white

Col Morrissey and Gen Wurtsmith's P-38Js are seen at Tadji during their inspection flight of 23 April 1944. The aircraft on the right was Wurtsmith's machine, which was marked with tri-colour propeller hubs – V Fighter Command's HQ marking. Morrissey's Lightning was the aircraft used by Dick Bong to break Eddie Rickenbacker's World War 1 scoring record (*Steve Ferguson*)

The 7th FS had developed a reputation for risqué nose art by mid-1944, and the example worn on squadron CO Capt Arland Stanton's favourite P-40N set the standard! It is shown here accompanied by one of his groundcrew (*Author*)

coral runways which the Fifth Air Force desperately needed for its heavy bombers.

On 7 May 16 P-40Ns of the 7th FS and 11 from the 8th FS took off on their first mission to Biak. After the Liberators had dropped their bombs on the island, Capt Elofson of the 8th FS sighted two Zekes – one of which had just dropped an aerial phosphorus bomb on a B-24. Elofson shot it down and the pilot bailed out, while his wingman, Lt Marion Felts, destroyed the second Zeke.

The 7th FS also entered the fray at that point, Capt Arland Stanton and his wingman both firing at another formation of Zekes, but apparently to no avail. The unit then tore into a large cluster of 'Oscars', and Capt Ed Peck and Lt Joel Paris both claimed a fighter destroyed. Paris quickly centred a second Ki-43 in his gunsight and shot it down, while Lt Fred

Lt Joel Paris rests on the wing root of his P-40N _Rusty_. The future 7th FS ace had claimed three kills by the time this photograph was taken, and he would boost his tally to nine after his unit re-equipped with the P-38J in September 1944. Paris finished the war as one of the 49th FG's senior pilots (_Author_)

This rare photograph shows Bob DeHaven in the cockpit of his P-40N shortly before the 7th FS converted to the P-38J in September 1944. The scoreboard on his Warhawk show ten kills, yet he was only credited with nine and no probables or damaged in the P-40 (_Author_)

Dick accounted for another. The latter soon sighted his second target for the day, which he later identified as a Nakajima Ki-44 'Tojo'. The Japanese fighter was in the process of outrunning six P-40s when Dick dived vertically on it to rake the stubby-winged aircraft from stem to stern. The tail section separated and the pilot bailed out. Dick climbed back up to 6000 ft, but was unable to find anyone to confirm his victory. The 'Tojo' was listed as a probable.

Bob DeHaven was leading his flight as top cover on this mission, and he was still overhead as the B-24s lumbered for home. He then spied a single aircraft flying a course parallel to the P-40s, but some distance below them. DeHaven slowly led his flight down until he was slightly below and directly behind the enemy aircraft. Identifying the Japanese insignia before he opening fire, the ace saw his foe burst into flames, roll on its back and crashed to become DeHaven's tenth victory – he was credited with destroying a Yokosuka D4Y1 'Judy' dive-bomber.

BACK TO BIAK

When the 7th FS returned to Biak on 16 May, its pilots soon found themselves in a scrap. Capt Owen Swartz had four flights stacked up to cover a pair of 71st Reconnaissance Squadron B-25s, but because of heavy cloud cover Swartz took two flights down to keep watch over the Mitchells. Unknown to him, his remaining top cover then became involved in a dogfight when flight leader Lt Lew Smith intercepted eight 'Oscars' and four Zekes that were heading his way 2000 ft above him. Smith considered attack to be his best form of defence, so he turned to meet the Zekes head-on. He scored multiple hits on one and the pilot bailed out.

With his wingman – Lt Nicanor Zuniga – still in formation behind him, Smith then returned to the fray and shot the left wing off a Zeke, which then tore a five foot gash in Zuniga's right wing. Despite his P-40N being thrown into a vicious spin, Zuniga not only recovered but was able to shoot down a Zeke which he found in front of him. By then Smith had been wounded in the right arm, but both he and Zuniga were able to make it home.

Lts John Fenimore and Laurence McInnis also took on two Japanese fighters, but their first pass at the Ki-43s inflicted no damage. Fenimore scored on the second, however, and the Japanese pilot was seen to leave his aircraft. McInnis also made a second pass and scored hits, and was seriously wounded in the process. He contemplated bailing out of his shot up P-40, but when he looked at the fighter's instrument panel the aircraft's engine seemed to running fine. McInnis strapped himself back into his seat and set about giving himself first aid. He had to cut a bandage with his good hand and apply a tourniquet to his right arm, before dressing a severe wound in his right leg. Despite being in great pain, McInnis managed to fly with one hand for two hours before making a successful belly landing.

'Green Flight' had become split up when flight leader 1Lt John Haher and his wingman were cut off by attacking 'Oscars'. Fred Dick and Warren Greczyn managed to turn into a pair of Ki-43s and shoot both of them down, but in their second pass on several other Japanese fighters they became separated and had to escape by diving for the deck. Greczyn found refuge with three retreating B-25s that he escorted home with

Maj Wallace Jordan, who succeeded Maj Jerry Johnson as 9th FS CO, became an ace in October 1944. Here, he obscures the serial of his P-38L-5 with a strategically placed hand in this portrait, taken at Biak soon after he 'made ace'. Note the metal case for his sunglasses tucked into the belt of his flying overall (*Author*)

Fenimore. As they started to head east, two surviving 'Oscars' approached, and as Fenimore was out of ammunition, Greczyn had to take care of the situation. He opened fire on one Ki-43, which rolled over and went into the sea. Not wishing to suffer a similar fate, the second 'Oscar' broke off and retreated. The fight was finally over. These actions yielded the 49th FG its final Warhawk victories.

In the early spring of 1944 Maj Bob McHale left the 8th FS for a staff job, being replaced by Maj Charles Peterson. The 7th FS's CO, eight-kill ace Maj Arland Stanton, completed an outstanding combat tour in May and then returned home, with Capt Ed Peck assuming command of the unit.

In mid April Maj Wally Jordan finally managed to acquire a mixed group of 24 refurbished P-38Js from the 475th FG, thus making the 9th FS a Lightning unit once again. They celebrated on 19 May during a mission to escort B-24s the 475 miles to Manokwari. While flying at 15,000 ft, 'Tojo' fighters were sighted, one of which was flying as top cover, with the others at around 2000 ft. Some distance off were four other 'Tojos', which were spotted by the two P-38 flights. Jordan reported;

'I took one shot from below at the high one, then dived on the other three. The one in front chandelled left, passing from my view, leaving a two-ship element slightly below and in front of me. I came in directly behind, took a shot at the element leader, then started firing at the wingman. He started burning violently, going into a turn to the left. My wingman, Lt Kirkland, saw him explode and we both saw the smoke in the jungle directly where the enemy aeroplane had hit. At this time I also saw a pilot going down in a 'chute. The parachute contained the element leader, who was shot down by Lt Kirkland – the pilot had bailed out while Lt Kirkland was shooting at him.'

Lt Willis Treadway also downed a 'Tojo'. Capt Del Moore managed to knock the canopy off another, but it was not seen to go down. Finally, Lt William Baxter took off after one of the Ki-44s and finally succeeded in shooting a wing off. The 9th FS was back in business.

PROTECTING BIAK

Following a two-week aerial bombardment, Allied forces captured the small island of Biak in early June, although Japanese bombers continued to attack the crucially important airfield every night. Gen Kenney was concerned because these raids were adversely affecting the schedule for the occupation of this badly-needed base by Fifth Air Force's heavy bombers. Reconnaissance information revealed that the Japanese were staging aircraft through a remote base at Babo village, in nearby western Irian Jaya. They were also thought to be assembling a large fighter force for an attack on Biak.

The 9th FS was assigned to attack Babo in a mission led by group CO, Lt Col David Campbell. Accordingly, at 0830 hrs on 3 June, 20 P-38s climbed to 15,000 ft and headed west. They crossed Vogelpop Peninsula and turned in the direction of their target. At 1130 hrs Campbell began to let down, and he soon spotted four 'Oscars' heading east among the clouds. Just behind them, flying in the opposite direction, were a further eight 'Oscars'. When the first four passed below Campbell, he called for the entire group to wheel right and attack.

As the enemy fighters disappeared into the clouds, the west bound formation of eight Ki-43s appeared in line with the banking P-38s. While Campbell and his flight continued after the flight of four, the remaining 16 Lightnings dropped their tanks and headed into the second formation of eight 'Oscars'.

The first to encounter them was 'Red Flight', led by Lt William 'Willy' Williams. Even though he was unable to shake off his empty drop tanks, Williams roared headlong into the enemy flight. On his first pass he overshot, but then sent an 'Oscar' down in flames on his second attack. Lt Charles McElroy continued after his leader's first target, caught it and shot it down. Lt Alex Datzenko also shot down a Ki-43, which fell not far from his leader's victim. A few seconds later, Williams roared back over the Babo airstrip to finish off a second 'Oscar'.

'White Flight', under Lt Don Lee, also roared over the base just as several 'Oscars' took off. Lee fired at three of them, but was forced to break off. Element leader Lt James Poston downed one over the aerodrome and Lt Robert Hamburger, seeing his first combat, was able to chalk up a probable on his pass.

'Green Flight', with Lt Edward Howes leading, took a toll of the 'Oscars' on the west side of the aerodrome, as both he and future five-kill

A typical servicing view at a field-type base – here, it is Biak, soon after the 49th FG's arrival. Refuelling aircraft at such sites often posed a problem to the long suffering groundcrews (*Steve Ferguson*)

Flight leader Capt Roger Farrell's *Island Dream* lived up to the 7th FS's high standards for nose art at Biak Island in August 1944 (*Steve Ferguson*)

ace Lt Warren Curton each shot one down before making another pass – a second fighter damaged by Curton was finished off by Lt Frederick Helterline. 'Blue Flight', however, was late for the big show, with only Lt Leslie Nelson managing to catch an 'Oscar' at the top of a loop. His P-38 was then badly holed by anti-aircraft fire.

As mentioned earlier, group CO Lt Col Campbell and his flight had gone off after the four 'Oscars' that were initially sighted. Now, over the aerodrome, they found themselves in the middle of at least a dozen enemy fighters. Campbell chased one heading east just over the tree-tops, while 8th FS CO Maj McHale sent another down in flames on his first pass. Lt Alfred Lewelling also got a kill, as did Lt Huard Norton. McHale then shot down an 'Oscar' with drop tanks, while Lewelling and Norton continued to fight. All three men knew that they had scored further hits, but this was impossible to confirm in the heat of battle.

Keen to claim his fifth kill, having scored four while leading the 8th FG's 36th FS in 1943-44, Lt Col David Campbell was last seen chasing a lone Ki-43 over Babo airfield. He was neither seen nor heard from again.

Again reinforcing the two motivating factors of most servicemen in-theatre, Lt Jack Fenimore *O'Riley's Daughter* was named after a popular drinking song (*Author*)

Lt Fenton Epling was killed when P-40N *Milk Wagon Express* crashed on 17 July 1944 after clipping parked aircraft at Hollandia during a beat-up of the airfield. He had taken the war-weary fighter aloft on a test flight following a recent refurbishment (*Steve Ferguson*)

For the time being senior 49th FG staff officer Maj Furlo Wagner took over command of the group.

PLAGUED!

This was a low time for the 49th FG. All three squadrons had moved to Biak and Mokmer airfields, where they encountered swarms of flies and mosquitoes which resulted in malaria becoming an ever-present threat. Pilots may have liked the hard coral runways, but groundcrews quickly learned to hate the fine coral dust that got into everything. Then, on the night of 12 June, the base was bombed yet again and 19 men were killed and 30 seriously injured. In the two-and-a-half years during which the group had been in action, this was its single worst loss of life.

By the 25th the 9th FS had arrived from Hollandia to complete the move to Biak, and the following day the group's P-40Ns attacked the island of Noemfoor without suffering any losses, or encountering aerial

opposition. In late June Maj Wagner returned to his group headquarters role and Lt Col George Walker was posted in from the US to become the new 49th FG CO. Capt Bobby Harrison assumed temporary command of the 7th FS at the same time, previous CO Capt Ed Peck being forced to stand down with a severe bout of malaria.

On 28 July the 9th FS got a mission it wanted – a 1200-mile round trip mission escorting B-24s sent to bomb Ambon Island, in the Dutch East Indies. On arrival over the target area at 10,000 ft, the P-38 pilots saw both fighters and bombers on the ground, but none opposed them. Two 'Val' dive-bombers were caught in the air, however, and they were pursued immediately by seven P-38s. Lt Jim Haislip took credit for the destruction of one, while wingman Lt Wade Lewis had only succeeded in knocking pieces off the second when it vanished into low-lying mist.

P-40N *Sugar* was assigned to Lt 'Willie' Drier of the 8th FS in 1943-44. Given command of the 8th in August 1944, he finished his tour a six-victory ace, having scored all of his kills with the P-38 (*Steve Ferguson*)

This P-38L, complete with command stripes around its tail booms, was flown by Maj Bob McComsey, 9th FS CO, from Biak in October 1944 (*Steve Ferguson*)

CHAPTER FIVE

This Nakajima Ki-43 'Oscar' was captured at Hollandia in June 1944 and made airworthy again by 49th FG groundcrews. It was named *RACOON Special* (*Steve Ferguson*)

Dubbed the 'Balikpapan Mob', these men of the 9th FS were amongst the pilots who helped V Fighter Command claim no fewer than 18 kills on 10 October 1944. Photographed at Biak, they are, back row from left to right, Capt Baker (V Fighter Command), Lt Col George Walker (49th FG CO), 2Lt Bob Hamburger, Maj Dick Bong (gunnery instructor), Capt Eddie Howes and 1Lts 'Jimmie' Haislip, Bob Wood, Warren Curton, A Hufford and Carl Estes. In the front row, from left to right, are Majs Robert McComsey (9th FS CO) and 'Wally' Jordan, 1Lt 'Mac' McElroy, Capt 'Wewak Willie' Williams and 1Lt Davis. The Lightning parked behind the pilots is P-38L-5 'Black 83', which Maj Jerry Johnson used to down an 'Oscar' and a 'Tojo' during a follow up mission to Balikpapan on 14 October (*John Stanaway*)

The Lightnings returned to Ambon on 4 August, and this time spotted two 'Oscars' just above the white cumulus clouds. They turned into the P-38s and Lt Charles McElroy caught the leader with a long burst. The Ki-43 tried to escape in a chandelle loop but McElroy caught it at the top and it exploded.

AN ALL-P-38 UNIT

On 28 August Capt Willie Drier took over command of the 8th FS. Three days later some of its pilots joined those of the P-38-equipped 475th FG for the long flight to Buayan aerodrome at Mindanao, in the southern Philippines. This mission marked the first penetration of the area by US fighters since 1942.

Two more long-awaited events occurred in early September when both the 7th and 8th FSs received Lightnings to mark the end of the Warhawk era for two of the most successful operators of the type in the Pacific. While these units struggled to keep weary hand-me-down P-38Js

airworthy, the 9th FS received brand new P-38L-1s and -5s to bring them right up to date.

There were further command changes in the 49th FG too, with Maj Jerry Johnson returning to become group Operations Officer and Maj Robert McComsey assuming command of the 9th FS. Maj Dick Bong, who was now V Fighter Command's senior gunnery instructor, also asked to be allowed to fly with the 49th FG, and he was assigned his own personal aircraft.

OIL STRIKES

It was at this time that Gen Kenney ordered strikes against Japanese oil production at the refineries at Balikpapan, on the eastern coast of Borneo. The first mission was to be flown on 10 October, with pilots from both the 9th FS and group HQ being led by Jordan and Bong. The day prior to the mission being flown, 15 P-38s assigned to the raid staged through Morotai to join up with 35th FG P-47Ds that were also escorting the B-24s to the target. Only one Lightning was forced to abort during the mission on the 10th, the remainder making the 850-mile one-way flight at 10,000 ft. Approaching the target, the fighters climbed to 15,000 ft and started to orbit Manggar, which was the area's principal airfield.

Bong soon spotted a twin-engined aircraft below him, and while Walker and the others kept an eye out for enemy fighters, he and his wingman, Capt Bob Baker, attacked what proved to be a Nakajima J1N 'Irving' twin-engined fighter. Bong opened fire as he caught the aircraft in a turn, then fired again and it rolled over on its back and burst into flames. The pair then rejoined the other P-38s.

Walker did his best to bring down an 'Oscar' but only damaged it. His wingman, Lt Warren Curton, was more successful, however. Jordan found another 'Irving', dived to attack and probably hit the enemy heavy fighter before its pilot was aware of the danger. He then climbed up and attacked two Ki-43s in conjunction with his wingman, Lt Willie Williams. After manoeuvring, Williams confirmed that Jordan had sent his victim plunging into the sea.

Lt Edward Howes, leading 'Green Flight', bounced an unsuspecting Zeke, and his point blank fire saw it explode. The P-38s then broke off combat and headed home. As they looked back, they could see a plume of black smoke some five miles high rising from the target.

Posted in from the US to replace Lt Col David Campbell, who was lost in action on 3 June 1944 in the last great dogfight over New Guinea, Lt Col George Walker remained in charge of the group until March 1945 (*John Stanaway*)

Maj Jerry Johnson begins his take-off roll at Biak in October 1944. Note the scoreboard ahead of the cockpit and the drop tank under each wing (*Steve Ferguson*)

The refineries were attacked again on the 14th, and this time the 35th FG preceded the 49th by about 15 minutes so as to provide a pre-mission sweep. Lt Col George Walker led 17 Lightnings, with Johnson in charge of 'White Flight', which included Maj Tommy McGuire, who was Bong's greatest rival for the title of top American ace. This flight was the first to reach the target area, and Johnson's account of what happened next provides a good description of the mutual support and professional fighter tactics employed by the 49th FG in the final year of the war;

'I entered the fight with Maj Thomas McGuire on my wing. I split-essed on an "Oscar" that was diving to attack the bombers. I made hits but over ran him. Maj McGuire nailed him with a dead astern burst and he began flaming. The pilot bailed out. I then attacked an "Oscar" from dead astern. The enemy aeroplane was flying across the bomber formation. I hit his fuselage and wings and he started smoking, and as I pulled up he burst into flames. Maj McGuire saw this aeroplane go down in flames. I then made a diving turn to the right and attacked a "Tojo" from dead astern. I rode up and blew him up before he was able to drop the two phosphorous bombs under his wings. Maj McGuire will also confirm this as a definite.

'As I regained altitude Maj McGuire peeled off to attack an unidentified enemy. I followed him through the attack and saw the aeroplane's tail section go to pieces first. Then the entire fuselage burst into flames. We were jumped, and in the melee I ended up with a "Tojo" firing at me from dead astern. I lost him by diving into the clouds just north-east of the target. Then I returned to the target area and made several deflection passes, but with nil results. Then three "Oscars" chased me out to sea for about five minutes. They fired repeated bursts but were not in effective range. When they turned back, I made a 180-degree turn and attacked the lead ship from above in a head-on pass. I saw a few hits and smoke, but the fighter dived into the clouds and I lost him. Total time in the air was 7 hours and 45 minutes.'

Lt Howard Oglesby, who was originally Johnson's wingman on this mission, was caught up in the whirl of the fight and downed two 'Oscars' himself. Jordan also shot down a Ki-43, while Lt Leslie Nelson performed the hat trick on three Zekes. Lt Ed Cooper was involved in the fight against the 'Tojos' when Johnson and McGuire made their attack and got one of them for himself.

The two long escort missions to Balikpapan had proved worthwhile. Bomb damage was extensive, and the fighter pilots from both the 49th and 35th FGs had been highly successful. But now the 49th was forced to begin a waiting game while the next stage of the Pacific war was launched.

PHILIPPINES FINALE

U S naval aircraft signalled the start of the campaign to re-take the Philippines with a series of bombing raids against Japanese installations on 10 October. There was a softening-up barrage on the 19th, and the following day US troops waded ashore. It was essential for the Americans to gain air superiority over the beachhead, and the 49th FG was among the first units selected to operate from Leyte.

Accordingly, 34 P-38s were ferried to Morotai on the 22nd to prepare for the 700-mile flight to Tacloban airfield. Among the lead pilots when the group departed on the morning of the 27th were CO Lt Col George Walker, V Fighter Command's Col Bob Morrissey and Majs Gerald Johnson and Dick Bong. The flight went well and the aircraft were on the ground by noon.

FIRST VICTORY OVER LEYTE

Morrissey and Bong were determined to score the first victory over Leyte, and they joined the first 9th FS patrol later that day. After bombing a target near Dulag, Lt Bob Wood, leading 'Yellow Flight', called 'Blue Flight' leader Lt Hal Oglesby and told him to regroup over the water before they ended the mission.

As the eight P-38s flew on, Wood reported engine trouble and went home, handing over his flight to Lt Bernie Krankowitz, who then sighted three 'Val' dive-bombers. Krankowitz wheeled around immediately. Closing rapidly, he opened fire, silencing the rear gunner. His wingman, Lt Arthur Hufford, also opened fire, and both 'Vals' went down in flames. Krankowitz chased after the third dive-bomber, and he succeeded in riddling it with gun fire before it disappeared into the overcast. Hufford found a fourth, and had just begun to fire, when his gun circuit malfunctioned and wasted all his ammunition.

Although the senior officers had not drawn first blood, they were certainly successful, as Johnson reported;

'We intercepted two "Oscars" at about 8000 ft. Maj Bong led the attack and overshot the aeroplane. I closed from rear astern and set him afire with a long burst. I then turned to rejoin the flight and observed an "Oscar" burst into flames just before striking the water. This aeroplane was destroyed by Col Robert Morrissey. Maj Bong destroyed an "Oscar" just off the coast. I saw the aeroplane right after it hit the water.

'I then observed Col Morrissey chasing a "Val". I closed with the "Val" from dead astern, and after a long burst set his engine on fire. As he glided in for a water landing, Col Morrissey shot the rear gunner. This aeroplane made a water landing and sank. I made one strafing pass before it sank.'

7th FS's FIRST KILL

The 7th FS (now flying P-38s) scored its first victory over the Philippines on the 28th after Capt John Haher's afternoon patrol encountered six 'Oscars' near Tacloban. They were able to approach without being seen, and as Haher began his attack, the leading Ki-43 rocked his wings,

suggesting that this might be a US Navy formation. However, when the aircraft turned Haher saw the red discs on their wings and immediately opened fire. The leading 'Oscar' split-essed and the Lightning pilot continued to fire until it hit the ground.

When Haher rejoined his flight, his second element was under attack. He chased another 'Oscar', but as he closed in his guns would not fire. The enemy fighter now began to escape, although it was quickly cut off by another P-38 that appeared to come down on it from nowhere. The latter machine was being flown by Dick Bong. He had been hunting for targets with Walker, Morrissey and Johnson, and now he set Haher's 'Oscar' on fire. He then pursued another Ki-43 carrying a bomb. The enemy pilot started diving away to the west, where he apparently released his bomb, only for it to wipe off his entire empennage.

By this stage of the battle Bong was accompanied only by Walker and Morrissey, and they now found a second flight of 17 'Oscars'. Bong advised Morrissey to climb for better radio range and call for reinforcements, before he and Walker dived on the Ki-43s. They tried to surprise two from behind, and Bong got a few strikes on one before the whole formation dropped their external fuel tanks and attacked the P-38s. Bong got hit in the left coolant radiator as he dived out and had to feather that engine, leaving Walker to escort him home.

Two 7th FS pilots scored victories on 29 October when Capt Bob DeHaven's flight became separated as they climbed through the overcast. The Warhawk ace emerged from the clouds to find himself alone. Undeterred, he cruised along until he saw some US Navy Hellcats chasing an 'Oscar', which they finished off. DeHaven then pursued another Ki-43

Joint top-scoring P-40 pilot in V Fighter Command, Capt Bob DeHaven continued his run of successes in combat when his unit transitioned onto the P-38L in the late summer of 1944 (*Author*)

As a P-40N and later a P-38J pilot with the 8th FS, Nelson Flack accounted for five Japanese fighters in 1943-44 (*Author*)

A 9th FS photo-call at Tacloban in late October 1944, just days after the unit had flown into the newly liberated airfield. Aces Jordan, Bong and Johnson stand side-by-side immediately below the nose of P-38L-1 44-23964, which had been Bong's mount during his attachment to the 49th FG as gunnery instructor throughout the Philippines campaign. The ace would claim six kills with the fighter between 10 October and 11 November 1944, taking his score to 36 victories. 44-23964 was subsequently lost while being flown by 49th FG Deputy Ops Officer Maj John Davis on 28 November, the pilot perishing when the fighter stalled in soon after taking off from Tacloban (*John Stanaway*)

in a high-speed chase which ended with the Japanese fighter plunging into the sea. A second flight led by Lt Elliott Dent also found a lone 'Oscar', and although three pilots fired at it, credit was given to Lt Milden Ohre. These two victories took the 49th FG's overall score to 500.

BATTLES OVER THE PHILIPPINES

The battle over the Philippines got under way in earnest during November. On the 1st Capt DeHaven led a patrol to Tacloban, which was then directed to Dulag where he shot down a Zeke making a strafing run on Allied shipping. Elsewhere, the 9th FS spent the day destroying three enemy aircraft some ten miles from Tacloban, Lt Cheatham Gupton accounting for two 'Vals' and Lt Howard Ogle an 'Oscar'.

Six-kill ace Capt Elliott Dent of the 7th FS who fought four Zekes alone on 1 November 1944 over Ormoc Bay and shot down three of them (*Steve Ferguson*)

Capt Ed Peck's 7th FS P-38J displays the unit's tail markings at Tacloban. The Bunyap had been the unit's insignia since early 1942 (*Steve Ferguson*)

That afternoon the 8th FS was patrolling over Tacloban when it encountered ten to fifteen hostile aircraft. The P-38 pilots quickly shot down two 'Oscars' and three Zekes, Capt Nelson Flack claiming one with a 90-degree deflection shot and Lt Walter Meyer causing a Ki-43 to explode in a head-on pass. Lt Nial Castle also fired at a Zeke in a 90-degree deflection shot, and followed this up by exploding a second Zeke in mid-air. Lt John Bodak made a head-on pass at an 'Oscar', which crashed and exploded.

Capt Elliott Dent had to fight for his life, however, and was fortunate to survive. He saw an enemy fighter heading over Ormoc Bay and went down after it. As he did so, four Zekes came out of the clouds to his right, so he turned into them. He reported;

'My flight had lost me in the clouds. I never saw them after that. I made a head-on pass at four enemy aircraft, firing a burst at the lead Nip. The outside men of the flight chandelled to the outside of the formation while the two in the centre split, one going up and one going down. From then on, for at least 15 or 20 minutes, which seemed like forever, I fought for my life. My memory is very hazy as to individual passes, but during the entire time I was either attacking or being attacked. As I would go in for a pass on one Nip, I'd see two others coming in to me. I'd fire short bursts, chase one and then pull into another before the second one could do any harm.

'On two occasions, to save myself, I had to split-ess at fairly low altitudes – one time pulling out just over the water as my aeroplane buffeted severely. This continued until only one Zeke was left. Two of the others had gone down in flames, while the third crashed into a mangrove swamp. At about 1000 to 2000 ft, as I closed on the fourth Zeke from the stern, he passed over a Jap destroyer and turned to the left. As I was just ready to fire, I must have been right over the destroyer for my right engine was shot out by what sounded like machine gun fire. I was blinded by the smoke and couldn't see even after the canopy was jettisoned.'

Dent bailed out of his P-38 and managed to evade searching Japanese vessels by not inflating his life-raft. Instead, he managed to find a coconut frond, which helped keep him afloat! Later that afternoon he was rescued by two Filipinos and eventually reached US naval forces, returning to his squadron on 15 November.

The tempo continued to increase with continuous missions being flown by the squadrons of the 49th on the 2nd, and some 26 Japanese aircraft being claimed destroyed during that day. Included in this haul were the first examples of the Mitsubishi J2M 'Jack' naval fighter encountered by the group, two falling to the 7th FS, along with a pair of 'Oscars' that were intercepted while escorting dive-bombers to Ormoc Bay. DeHaven tangled with one of the 'Jacks' as he left the area, the ace having to climb hard in his P-38L to reach it. Once at the same level as the J2M, he found the aircraft to be very fast. DeHaven blasted it from point-blank range and the 'Jack' literally exploded in front of him.

The 8th FS ran into at least 20 Zekes and 'Oscars' on their first mission of the day, providing fighter cover for ships moored in Ormoc Bay. Capt William Drier had a field day with an 'Oscar' and two Zekes destroyed, and veteran Lt Marion Felts got two Zekes before being shot down. He was covered by Lt Tom Holstein as he parachuted safely down. Capt Phil

Kriechbaum was not so fortunate, as he was killed when his fighter was destroyed in an ambush by three well flown 'Oscars'.

The 9th FS also encountered heavy enemy opposition to its patrol over Ormoc Bay on the 2nd, but accounted for ten of the attacking Zekes and 'Oscars'. Lts Thomas Hamilton, William Huisman and James Poston each scored doubles, but Huisman's triumph would be short lived. As he landed back at base, another P-38 ran into the rear of his aircraft, causing it to slide down the runway in flames. Huisman was pulled from the burning wreckage but later succumbed to his injuries.

DeHAVEN'S LAST

Bob DeHaven scored his last victory on 4 November. Scrambled to intercept enemy aircraft over Tacloban early that morning, he sighted three 'Vals' and three fighters. He went after them, and as he approached one of the fighters broke away. DeHaven slid in behind him and stayed on the Zeke's tail until he was within range. The Lightning pilot then opened fire and the naval fighter became victory number 14. DeHaven was ordered home shortly afterwards.

Dick Bong flew his last mission with the 49th exactly one week later when, accompanied by Morrissey, Johnson, Haher and Lt Bill Minto, he escorted a C-47 on a supply drop to Homonhon Island. Sighting six Zekes, the P-38 pilots began climbing. Johnson went after one and it exploded under his fire, while Bong chased down two Zekes and Johnson duly saw both of them crash – victories 35 and 36 for the USAAF's leading ace.

While patrolling over their base later that day, a flight of 7th FS P-38s sighted three 'Tojos' above them. The Lightnings rapidly climbed to

Capt Bob DeHaven was 7th FS top scorer with 14 victories, claiming nine flying the Warhawk and five in the Lightning. Here, he poses with his elaborately marked P-38L (serial unknown) at Linguyan in June 1945. All of his aircraft were marked with the number 13, this particular machine being DeHaven's mount during his brief second tour in the Pacific in mid 1945. Note the dive-bombing guides in the form of black stripes marked on the wing leading edge inboard of the port engine

15,000 ft – well above the enemy – and Lts Fernley Damstrom, Fred Dick and Harold Harris took care of all three Ki-44s.

Early on the 14th Lt Robert Goodwin of the 8th FS caught a Zeke over Tacloban, the young pilot putting on a show for those watching on the ground as he despatched the fighter with little trouble. Two days later the 9th FS caught a formation of 'Oscars' trying to attack airstrips south of Tacloban. Lts Cheatham Gupton, Warren Fowler and Jack Lewis each shot down two Ki-43s, while Lt Warren Curton got the seventh.

Lt Edward Glascock and rookie Lt Gerald Triplehorn took off early on the 18th and encountered a lone Zeke, which Glascock finished off with a flourish. As they continued their patrol, they met four brand new Nakajima Ki-84 'Frank' fighters spoiling for a fight. Glascock knew immediately it was going to take all of his skill to survive, and he managed to down one a 'Frank' before escaping. Triplehorn never had a chance, the rookie crashing to his death in the nearby mountains.

The morning of the 24th saw a 7th FS patrol encounter the enemy when Lt Jim O 'Neill was vectored onto a single Zeke, which he quickly shot down. The patrol then joined other P-38s in combat with various enemy aircraft types. O'Neil and his flight attacked some 'Tonys', and one was quickly sent down in flames. As O'Neil dived away, another Ki-61 crossed his sights and he fired at it, but it was not confirmed as destroyed. Two Zekes were subsequently shot down before the patrol went home.

Capt Robert Aschenbrener had just returned to the 8th FS from leave in the US, and had barely completed a handful of familiarisation flights in the P-38, when he was thrown into the action on the 24th. Flying on Capt Bill Drier's wing during a patrol over Caragara Bay, he sighted a single

Lt Fernley Damstrom was an eight-kill 7th FS P-38 ace who claimed all of his kills between 2 November and 20 December 1944 over the Philippines. He was killed on 10 April 1945 when he suffered engine failure while taking off from Laoag airstrip, Luzon, in fully fuelled P-38L-5 44-25327. The aircraft flipped over and crashed on its back on a nearby beach, breaking the young ace's neck (*Steve Ferguson*)

'Tony' and quickly celebrated his return to combat by blowing off its tail. As the patrol continued, Drier and Aschenbrener became separated from the main element as they went after some Zekes. Each downed one. Aschenbrener then made a pass at a 'Tony' as it dived by him, Drier seeing it burst into flames and the pilot bail out.

Minutes later Aschenbrener chased another 'Tony', but only one of his guns was working so he closed to within 50 yards before firing. Lt Jim Franks of the 7th FS saw the 'Tony' split apart and burst into flames. It was now Drier's turn again, and he set another 'Tony' on fire, before attacking another head-on which disappeared into clouds with smoke and flames pouring out of it. With four claims for Aschenbrener and three for Drier, it was time to go home.

Lts Cecil Archer and Oliver Atchison both got Zekes on the 26th, and an hour later Lt Cheatham Gupton finished off an 'Oscar'. Two days later Aschenbrener got another 'Tony' over Ormoc Bay and on the 29th it was also the location of kills by Lts Warren Curton and Wade Lewis of the 9th FS – both shot down Zekes. 8th FS pilot Lt Thomas Holstein caught a lone 'Dinah' near Ragatoon on the 30th to end a record-breaking month for the 49th FG.

CONVOY COVER

With Japanese aerial strength now depleted, the next priority was to provide cover for convoys and ground forces as they advanced through the Philippines chain. The action began on 5 December when P-38s of the 9th FS supported troop transports sailing into Ormoc Bay. Eight 'Val' dive-bombers, with escorting 'Oscars', were intercepted while attempting

Bob 'Ash' Aschenbrener completed two tours with the 8th FS, flying some 272 missions in P-40s between May 1943 and mid 1944. Having claimed three kills in his first tour, Aschenbrener returned to combat just as the Philippine campaign was getting into full swing. On 24 November 1944 he flew his first combat mission in a P-38 and claimed four kills to 'make ace'. By the time he was given command of the 7th FS on 21 February 1945, he had increased his score to ten. Maj Aschenbrener is seen here with his P-38L in the spring of 1945 (*Author*)

to bomb the convoy, and the Lightning pilots quickly sent down three D3As and dispersed the rest. Lt Ernest Ambort and Flt Off Henry Hammett also added an 'Oscar' apiece to their dive-bomber kills, while Lt Charles McElroy downed the third 'Val'.

Later that day a 9th FS patrol encountered more 'Oscars' attempting to bomb the convoy. The Japanese pilots hastily headed for the clouds, although Lt Warren Curton did manage to shoot one down before they all disappeared. The next day, while the 7th FS was covering the same convoy, its pilots intercepted a 'Lily' bomber that was scouting around and Lt James Jarrell shot it down.

D-Day for the invasion of Ormoc Bay came on 7 December – the third anniversary of the attack on Pearl Harbour. All three 49th FG squadrons were active that day, and together scored 23 victories. The first kills fell to the command flight as its patrolled over the beachhead at 12,000 ft. Jerry Johnson reported;

'Col Morrissey led the attack, but the "Oscars" made a hard right turn into him and he was unable to get a good shot. I closed on the last "Oscar" and shot him down in flames. I then dived after the other two and then followed them in a climb. As they turned sharply to the right, I had good deflection shots and was able to get both of them. These two "Oscars" crashed into the water within a few hundred feet of each other.

'I rejoined the flight and followed Col Morrissey in an attack on six "Helen" bombers. I fired into the left wingman of the left V of the formation. He began smoking and broke away from the formation. I made a front quarter pass on him as he went down. This aeroplane crashed in flames.'

Capt Joel Paris poses with his P-38L *Georgia Belle* at the end of the war in the Pacific. The 7th FS ace scored his final victory on 6 March 1945 – one of the last claimed by the 49th FG. Paris remained in the air force post-war, eventually retiring as a colonel in 1970 (*Author*)

The 7th FS ran into a variety of hostile aircraft, Lt Fernley Damstrom accounting for two Ki-45 'Nick' fighters and Lt Milden Mathre getting both a 'Nick' and an 'Oscar'. Damstrom returned to score a third victory for the day when he shot down a Zeke 52. Two further 'Nicks' were downed that morning by Lts Joel Paris and Kenneth Markham.

The 8th FS then got in on the act, with Lt Robert Campbell shooting down an 'Oscar' and, later in the day, a Mitsubishi Ki-21 'Sally' bomber. Lt Walter Meyer also contributed a Zeke to the day's tally.

The 9th FS flew two missions, claiming a bag of three Zekes and an 'Oscar'. Victors were Lts Ernest Ambort, Charles McElroy, Troy Smith and Capt Willis Treadway. Late in the afternoon Lt Noah Williams got a 'Lily'.

On the 11th a 8th FS formation, led by Aschenbrener, sighted a convoy of Japanese naval vessels and supply ships, escorted by at least 30 fighters. Aschenbrener destroyed a 'Tojo', while Lts George Reed and Francis Hill accounted for Zeke 52s. Lt James McCrary scored the 7th FS's only victory of the day when he destroyed a Zeke 15 miles west of Leyte. The following day, Lt Joel Paris was leading a search mission in the same area when they encountered 'Betty' bombers. Paris and Lts Robert Decker and Warren Greczyn each downed a bomber apiece.

COVER FOR MINDORO LANDINGS

While covering the landings on Mindoro Island on 15 December, a flight of 7th FS P-38s clashed with eight Zeke 52s. Flight leader Lt Fernley Damstrom claimed two kills, while Lts Oliver Atchison, Milden Mathre and James Jarrell got one each. There were no further victories until the

18th, when Capt Willie Williams shot down a lone 'Dinah' ten miles south of the Mindoro beachhead.

Many of the Zekes now being encountered were improved 52 models, which boasted better armament and protective armour for both the pilot and the fighter's fuel tanks. They were also faster, and with wings made of heavier gauge material. Yet these improvements did not prevent dozens of them being destroyed during the Philippines campaign.

Lt Joel Paris was flying a convoy protection mission on 20 December when he sighted Zeke 52s over Mindoro. He soon ran into trouble, as he later reported;

'I saw a Zeke firing at me from "five o'clock". I turned into him and a piece of canopy about six inches in diameter blew off near the side of my head. My goggles and helmet were ripped off my head and flew out the hole – I just managed to save my helmet, but lost my goggles. Another Nip came in from behind, so I split-essed. I levelled off at 5000 ft, dropped my external gas tanks and started to climb back up, when Lt Mathre called me to turn right. I did, and shot a Zeke off his tail. I last observed the Nip smoking. I dived out again because of attacks from the rear. I finally got back up to 9000 ft, where I shot a Zeke 52 down from "six o'clock". The pilot of the Zeke bailed out but failed to reach the ground alive.'

Lt James Jarrell got two Zeke 52s in the same fight, and Lt Fernley Damstrom shot down an 'Oscar'.

The following afternoon Capt Aschenbrener led a flight covering a Mindoro convoy. A single Zero was sighted, with four Navy Hellcats on its tail. It rolled a couple of times, split-essed and started climbing away from the Navy fighters – right into Aschenbrener's sights for his tenth victory. By then, however, the Japanese had severely damaged the convoy, with one ship suffering three kamikaze hits and smoking heavily. The 8th FS stayed overhead as long as they could, but eventually a lack of fuel forced the Lightnings to land on Mindoro's San Jose strip.

The next day, while the flight was returning to Tacloban, Lt Francis Hill latched onto a solitary 'Tony', which he watched crash into the water.

RETURN TO CLARK FIELD

With the capital of Manila heavy damaged, Gen Kenney was determined to finish off Japanese air power in Luzon. Although it had been all but destroyed by the Japanese in 1941, Clark Field remained their primary base in the region, as it had been for the US Army Air Corps pre-war. Kenney suspected Japanese air power would still be concentrated there, so he planned a massive raid for Christmas Day, with B-24s being escorted by a large number of P-38s.

As a result, all squadrons of the 49th FG were involved in the air battle which took place on the 25th, fighting alongside units from the 475th FG. The 49th would score 15 victories in what would be the group's final large-scale aerial engagement with the Japanese. Sweeping over Clark Field, the 8th FS scored three victories as Lts James Atkinson, Harold Bechtold and Robert Goodwin each claimed kills. Capt Aschenbrener was hit by ground fire during the same attack, and after crash-landing his fighter he managed to evade the enemy and reach Huk natives, who returned him to his unit some four weeks later.

The 9th FS also claimed three kills when a trio of 'Tojos' were destroyed by Lts Alfred Lewelling (two) and Dan Holladay. The day belonged to the 7th FS, however, whose pilots managed to knock down eight of the twenty hostile fighters they encountered. All were single victories, and all were over Zeke 52s. They were credited to Lts Robert Decker, James Franks, Robert Klemmedson, James McHenry, Albert Meschino, William Minto, Joel Paris and William Thompson.

Another escort mission was flown to Clark the next day, but this time there was a shortage of targets for the P-38s. Indeed, only the 8th FS scored for the 49th, with victories being recorded by Lts Nial Castle and Sammy Pierce. They were both involved in a dogfight which included Maj Tommy McGuire, the 475th FG ace who was doing his utmost to pass Bong's 40 victories. Lt Castle was credited with two Zekes, while Pierce was involved in a wild battle, as the following extracts from his combat report indicate;

'I was flying No 4 ship in Lt Holstein's flight. We got a call from above, and a few seconds later 12 came down. Drop tanks, started turn, climb at high speed and up into a flight of three that were trying to get behind Holstein and the two behind him. Middle Nip met me head-on and would not break, and I thought he would try to ram me. He dropped his nose and tried to fire at me. I gave him a burst that hit his engine, which gave off a blue flame, and pieces fell off – my hits walked right on back over the ship as we closed. I lost sight of him as I pulled over.

'Pulled up and tried to find my wingman and rejoin the flight. There were four Nips going after Holstein's flight, which was just below me. I rolled over and went down on a "Tojo" that began firing at the No 3 man. He started to burn when I hit him, and pieces were observed to break off. He rolled his belly up, and it gave me a broadside shot with no deflection. The aeroplane went down trailing smoke and fire – he was seen to crash.

'I had lost the flight. I saw five Nips going down for the bomber formation so I followed but could not get in range. I saw Maj McGuire shoot down one in flames, and another that crashed behind the tail of the bomber formation. This time I was getting in range of five Nips. I went after the No 2 man, but could not get a shot, so I pulled around after No 1 man. Pulled up and gave him a burst – missed. Second shot – missed. The third put him into flames.

'I was then jumped by three Nips at 10,000 ft, so I went into long shallow dive at full power, then up into high climb. I pulled away from them, then one broke off and went in the opposite direction. I had the advantage in both speed and altitude. Went down on them and No 2 rolled and went under me. I went after the No 1 man, and gave a burst which hit his engine. No 2 man had pulled around and was firing at me. "Clover Flight" took him off me. I continued to follow the No 1 man. He went into overcast, then pulled out and gave me a good shot. I hit him around the wing roots and he rolled over and dived into clouds, burning, from 2000 ft.

'Climbed to 6000 ft and saw eight to ten P-38s chasing one Nip – shot, missed and overran. Others not in range. I got in front of them and gave the enemy a long burst – he started to burn (this Zeke 52 had been McGuire's target). Pulled up and joined Maj McGuire as his wingman.'

The 7th FS's Lt Milden Mathre stands with his crew chief alongside their P-38L-1 soon after scoring his fifth victory – a Zeke 52 over Clark Field – on New Year's Day 1945. The aircraft featured the nickname *'GOAT NOSE'* beneath the cockpit, as well as a caricature of its pilot (*Steve Ferguson*)

A 7th FS P-38J rests between missions at Tacloban in the autumn of 1944, its unit-inspired blue and white spinners being clearly visible. The spacious hard standing of this key Philippine airfield seems a long way from the jungle strips occupied by the 49th FG for much of its war in the Pacific (*Steve Ferguson*)

The result was one 'Tojo' confirmed and three Zeke 52s confirmed, and one probably destroyed, for Pierce, making him an ace with seven kills.

The end of the month saw all three squadrons move to Mindoro, where the bases were superior to Tacloban.

The 49th FG returned to Clark Field as escorts for B-24s on New Year's Day, with Paris leading a 7th FS flight that encountered five Zeke 52s. They immediately went into a Lufbery circle, and he tried to break it up by bringing his flight in on them from the opposite direction. It did not work. Later, the flight ran into a scattered formation of Zeke 52s, and Paris was able to down one and Lt Milden Mathre got another to become an ace.

The 8th FS, meanwhile, had stayed with the Liberators until they had dropped their bombs. The unit then went looking for hostile fighters. Lt Irwin Dames knocked down the No 4 man of an 'Oscar' flight that was soon found in the area, while Lt Francis Hill dived through the clouds to dispose of a Zeke 52 which was trailing his partner. On the way home, Lt Nial Castle sighted a lone 'Nick' twin-engined fighter and, using clouds for cover, crept up and shot it down in flames.

The 49th had to wait until 16 January for its next victim. A 7th FS flight was briefed to escort a Navy PBY, but the mission was called off due to bad weather and the Lightning pilots were left to find their way home in foul weather. En route, they sighted an Aichi E13A 'Jake' floatplane, which Lt Albert Meschino destroyed. The weather was so bad that the P-38 pilots could not find their way home, forcing Lt Huie Manes to belly-land in shallow water and Meschino to bail out. Both men were rescued by Negros tribesmen.

Three days later two 9th FS pilots encountered one of the Japanese Navy's new Yokosuka P1Y 'Frances' bombers. Rookie pilots Lts Troy

Smith and John Forgey easily overtook the aircraft, which was trying to remain hidden just above the water. Forgey was credited with its destruction.

Capt Jim Costley was a 7th FS flight leader during the recapture of the Philippines. He is pictured here with his aircraft *Winnie* (*Steve Ferguson*)

MISSIONS TO FORMOSA

After strafing missions to Luzon, February 1945 brought what was to become a regular pattern – sweeps of the island of Formosa. Towards the end of the month the squadrons moved to Linguyan, which, compared to their former bases, proved to be a huge complex. Through February and into March, there had been no aerial opposition, but pilots continued to fly missions over Formosa and islands like Negros and Cebu. Most sorties took the form of bomber escort, but some combined strafing and bombing which resulted in several casualties.

On 6 March the 7th FS escorted B-25s to Hainan Island, in the South China Sea, the unit being led by Capt Fred Dick. Over the target area, some 15 to 20 Zeke 52s began to attack the B-25s, and Dick immediately shot one down. He then made two passes against fighters pursuing the medium bombers, and as one of the attackers broke off, Dick latched onto its tail and blew it up.

Near the end of the mission, support was provided for a B-24 with half its tail shot away. Lt Paris was also on the mission, and he had to knock a Zeke off his wingman's tail. Both Paris and Dick later called the opposing Japanese pilots experienced and very aggressive. Three other Zeke 52s fell to the 7th FS, claimed by Capt Dwight Henderson and Lts Dewey Renick and George Spruill.

A number of 8th FS aircraft had been posted 20 miles out to sea to provide cover for casualties on the return leg of the mission, and when a US Navy PBM rescue aircraft reported that it was looking for a downed

The 7th FS's last ace was Capt Fred Dick (left), who is seen here with squadronmates Capts Jim Keck and Dick Gachan at Linguyan not long after the 6 March 1945 mission that had seen Dick become an ace when he downed two Zeke 52s (*Steve Ferguson*)

P-38L 44-27120 of the 8th FS is seen in flight with five-round rocket rails (dubbed Christmas trees by the pilots) beneath each wing and a single drop tank (*Steve Ferguson*)

B-25 crew, Lts Irwin Dames and Jack Page volunteered to escort the flying boat. The weather got progressively worse, as did communication between the aircraft, and as the P-38 pilots prepared to head for home, they sighted a lone Zeke heading for Hainan. After a brief chase Page caught it and shot it down.

ATTACKS WITH NAPALM

As Japanese troops on Luzon were pushed further inland, it became more difficult for the American troops to dig them out. In March, one of the 49th's primary missions was to bomb enemy positions with napalm – basically a 150-gallon drop tank filled with 140 gallons of jellied gasoline with an impact detonator. This weapon was found to be highly effective during the final phase of the campaign in the Philippines.

The second week in March saw a change in command, with Col George Walker being succeeded as 49th FG CO by Lt Col Jerry Johnson. By then the latter was regularly leading fighter sweeps along the Chinese coast which would eventually go all the way to Hong Kong.

The 8th FS scored its last victory on 15 March when Capt Willie Drier was covering a rescue mission by a Navy PB4Y along the western shore line of the Formosa Straits. He chased a 'Tojo' with his wingman, rookie Lt James Ward, and as they closed, another Ki-44 appeared in Drier's path and he took a snap shot at it, knocking pieces off the fighter. Ward subsequently shot down the first 'Tojo'. The 9th FS scored its final victory on 2 April while escorting B-24s sent to bomb Hong Kong airfields. The unit was accompanied by two combat veterans – Jerry Johnson and his friend Capt Jim Watkins, the latter having just returned to the 49th for a second combat tour. Johnson's account of the mission is typically brief and concise;

'We arrived over the target at 1300 hrs and observed six B-24s drop bombs on a warehouse in Hong Kong. No fires resulted. At 1340 hrs we sighted two "Tojos" 10 to 15 miles north of Hong Kong at 8000 to 10,000 ft and gave chase. Diving from 12,000 to 14,000 ft, I made a dead astern attack on one "Tojo" and saw 20 mm and 0.50-cal shells explode and tear pieces out of the left wing root. I returned for a second pass, and from 20 degrees deflection put 20 mm and 0.50-cal "slugs" in its engine and fuselage section. He went into a spin and crashed in a dry river bed about ten miles north of Hong Kong.'

Capt Willie Drier of the 8th FS was another late war ace, although he had flown P-40s with the unit since the autumn of 1943. Made CO of the unit in August 1944, he claimed six Japanese fighters flying P-38J/Ls between 2 and 24 November during the fierce dogfights over Ormoc Bay (*Author*)

Watkins fired at two 'Tojos' but did not know until he returned to base that 'Lt Williams in "Blue Flight" had observed the "Tojo" that I attacked continue his split-ess right on down into Mother Earth's bosom'. Lt Walter Koby was also victorious, downing a single 'Oscar'.

THE FINAL VICTORY

By April 1945 even opportunities for ground strafing had become limited. Visits to Formosa continued, and it was here that the 49th FG would score its final aerial victory of the war.

Maj George Laven had joined the HQ flight in March 1945, and his ambition had been to score the one victory in the air that would make him an ace – at least in his eyes. He had claimed four unconfirmed kills in Alaska with the 54th FS/55th FG in 1942-43, and now went to Formosa as often as possible. Laven virtually put the island's small gauge railway system out of commission, but that was not what he wanted. On 26 April he spotted two aircraft in the mist over Kato village. One was a 'Val' and the other was a big four-engined Kawanishi H8K 'Emily' flying boat. Laven selected it as his target, closing to within point blank range before opening fire. The big aircraft burst into flames and crashed.

On 16 May the 49th FG participated in a major napalm raid on Ipo, where some 4700 Japanese soldiers had gathered. The Ipo reservoir was

Maj Jim Watkins returned to the 49th FG in February 1945 and flew this brand new P-38L-5 44-26407, which he named *Charlcie Jeanne* like his previous P-38H-1 in New Guinea in 1943. He shot down a 'Tojo' for his 12th victory on a mission to Hong Kong with Lt Col Jerry Johnson on 2 April 1945 (*Ferguson*)

Flamboyantly decorated P-38L-5 44-25568 *Itsy Bitsy II* was the personal aircraft of Maj George Laven, who claims that he used it to 'wreck the railroad system on Formosa'. Laven also scored his 'fifth' aircraft destroyed in the same area on 26 April 1945 (*Author*)

Pilots brief for a mission over Luzon, in the Philippines, in May 1945. The group was based at Linguyan Field, also on Luzon (*Steve Ferguson*)

one of Manila's primary water sources, and Gen MacArthur had decreed that its capture was a top priority. Some 480 fighters laden with napalm carried out the attack.

Mission tempo slackened as summer arrived, the 49th FG being told that it would be moving to Okinawa for the invasion of Japan. There was a final change of command in July when Lt Col Clayton Tice succeeded Jerry Johnson. A 49th FG veteran, Tice looked forward to leading the group in combat over Japan, and he immediately began preparing for the move to Okinawa. But it was not to come. The bombing of Hiroshima and Nagasaki had seen to that. For the 49th FG the war was over.

Lt Col Clayton Tice poses with his P-38L in the spring of 1945 soon after becoming the last wartime CO of the 49th FG (*Author*)

Lt Col Johnson (centre, back row) poses with fellow 49th FG HQ pilots at Linguyan after he had scored his final kill on 1 April 1945. Flanking the group CO in the back row are Majs George 'Choo-Choo' Laven (possibly five kills) and Clay Tice, while in the front row, from left to right, are Capt Bob DeHaven (14 kills), Maj 'Wally' Jordan (six kills) and Capt James 'Duckbutt' Watkins (12 kills). The latter pilot had also claimed his final victory on 1 April 1945. Forming the backdrop to this group shot is Jerry Johnson's final Lightning – an unidentified P-38L-5 which was appropriately named *Jerry*. The fighter boasts his full tally of 25 kills, which included his RAAF Wirraway and two Aleutian 'Rufes' which Johnson always claimed, but which were not officially recognised by the USAAF (*John Stanaway*)

THE RECKONING

And what a war it had been. From a very green, ill equipped and poorly-trained unit, the 49th had learned from the Java survivors, and through its own hard-won experience, how to defeat the Japanese enemy. Its pilots also had to fight the weather and the harsh environment to survive New Guinea. Yet, they had become the best there was in Fifth Air Force, claiming a record 668 aerial victories.

APPENDICES

APPENDIX 1

VICTORIES SCORED BY THE 49th FG

Headquarters	28
7th Fighter Squadron	178
8th Fighter Squadron	207
9th Fighter Squadron	254
Total	667

APPENDIX 2

49th FG ACES

This list only details pilots who claimed five or more kills while flying with the 49th FG

Maj Richard I Bong (9th FS)	40[1]	Maj William C Drier (8th FS)	6
Lt Col Gerald R Johnson (9th FS and HQ)	22	1Lt Robert L Howard (8th FS)	6
1Lt James P Hagerstrom (8th FS)	14.5[2]	Maj Wallace R Jordan (9th FS and HQ)	6
1Lt John D Landers (9th FS)	14.5[3]	1Lt Donald W Meuten (8th FS)	6
Capt Robert M DeHaven (7th FS)	14	Capt Ralph H Wandrey (9th FS)	6
Capt James A Watkins (9th FS and HQ)	12	Capt Ellis W Wright (HQ)	6
Capt Robert W Aschenbrener (8th FS)	10	2Lt Ernest J Ambort (9th FS)	5
Capt Ernest A Harris (8th FS)	10	2Lt Nial K Castle (8th FS)	5
Capt Andrew J Reynolds (9th FS)	9.333[4]	1Lt Warren D Curton (9th FS)	5
1Lt Grover E Fanning (9th FS)	9	1Lt William C Day (8th FS)	5
Capt Joel B Paris III (7th FS)	9	Capt Frederick E Dick (7th FS)	5
Capt Robert H White (8th FS)	9	1Lt Marion C Felts (8th FS)	5
1Lt James B Morehead (8th FS)	8[5]	Capt Nelson D Flack (8th FS)	5
1Lt John G O'Neill (9th FS)	8	1Lt Cheatham W Gupton (9th FS)	5
Maj Arland Stanton (7th FS)	8	Capt William F Haney (9th FS)	5
1Lt Fernley H Damstrom (7th FS)	7	1Lt A T House (7th FS)	5
1Lt Sammy A Pierce (8th FS)	7	2Lt Milden E Mathre (7th FS)	5
Capt Elliott E Dent (7th FS)	6	Capt Robert H Vaught (9th FS)	5

Notes
1) 21 kills scored during 9th FS assignments and the balance with V Fighter Command HQ after leaving 49th FG
2) 1 kill with 334th FIS, 1 kill with 335th FIS and 6.5 kills with 67th FBS in Korean War
3) 1 kills with 55th FG, 1 kills with 357th FG and 3.5 kills with 78th FG after leaving 49th FG
4) 0.333 kills with 20th PS(P) and 4 kills with 17th PS(P) before joining 49th FG
5) 2 kills with 17th PS(P) before joining 49th FG and 1 kill with 1st FG after leaving 49th FG

COLOUR PLATES

1

P-40E (serial unknown) 'Yellow 57' of Capt George E Kiser, 8th FS, Strauss Field, Darwin, May 1942

'King' Kiser, considered by many contemporaries to be the best fighter pilot in the south-west Pacific in 1942, was already an ace when he joined the 8th FS, having destroyed two enemy aircraft in the Philippines on the third day of the war and three more during the Java campaign. His P-40E in the 8th FS, photographed at Darwin in May 1942, carried his personal lion ('king of the jungle') artwork and seven red dots representing his victory total at the time – it would also eventually boast a red forward spinner denoting that the aircraft's pilot was a Philippines/Java veteran. The fighter also reportedly had its two outboard machine guns removed to save weight and improve manoeuvrability. Kiser scored nine victories in the Pacific. He returned to combat in 1944, flying P-47s in the European theatre, but did not add to his score.

2

P-40E (serial unknown) 'White 80' of Capt Joseph J Kruzel, 9th FS, Livingstone Field, Darwin, spring 1942

The green dragon displayed on the nose of this machine indicated that Joe Kruzel led 'Dragon Flight'. He had joined the 49th PG in early 1942 after having scored three victories over Java flying a dragon-marked P-40E with the 17th PS – he did not score with the 49th. Kruzel went on to become CO of the Eighth Air Force's 361st FG in England in 1944, and 'made ace' with the group after scoring a further 3.5 kills flying P-47Ds and P-51B/Ds.

3

P-40E (serial unknown) 'White 44' of Lt Monty Eisenberg, 8th FS, Strauss Field, Darwin, June 1942

Eisenberg was one of the Java veterans who came to the 49th in 1942. He was involved in many scraps over Darwin but was not credited with any kills. This aircraft was written off in a crash-landing at Strauss Field on 13 June after it was shot up by a 3rd *Kokutai* Zero over Darwin harbour. Nursing the crippled machine back to base, Eisenberg ended up hanging by his seatbelt straps when the fighter flipped over onto its back after ground-looping. He scrambled out from beneath the P-40 with cuts and bruises.

4

P-40E-1 41-24872 'White 94' of Capt Robert H Vaught, 9th FS, Livingstone Field, Darwin, summer 1942

A former enlisted cavalryman, Vaught was a member of the original cadre of 9th PS pilots who sailed for Australia in January 1942. He scored three confirmed victories in P-40s, then achieved acedom with two more in 1943 after the squadron had converted to P-38s. Vaught's *"Bob's Robin"* was one of four sharkmouthed P-40Es in the 9th FS. The name was repeated on the starboard side of the fuselage, which showed considerable signs of patching and repainting.

5

P-40E-1 41-25163 'White 74' of Capt Sidney S Woods, 9th FS, Livingstone Field, Darwin, summer 1942

Woods, another original member of the 9th PS, was injured in a landing accident in late March 1942 and was assigned this aircraft upon his return to duty after a month's medical leave. He failed to score any victories with it, however, although he did score twice in P-38s before completing his tour in the summer of 1943. Woods returned to combat with the Eighth Air Force's 4th FG (as its deputy group CO), claiming five further victories during a single combat in March 1945. He was shot down while strafing shortly thereafter and finished the war as a PoW.

6

P-40E-1 41-25164 'White 75' of Capt Ben S Irvin, 9th FS, Livingstone Field, Darwin, August 1942

Senior flight leader Ben Irvin was known as 'Bitchin' Ben' to his squadronmates, and his aircraft displayed a large Pegasus emblem on its fuselage, in addition to the name *"THE REBEL"* on its nose. Irvin's only two victories were scored over Java in February 1942.

7

P-40K-1 42-46288 'Yellow 13' of Lt A T House, 7th FS, Port Moresby, March 1943

House may well have been the 49th FG's most decorated pilot, for he was awarded the Distinguished Service Cross for saving his squadron CO on 14 March 1942 (when he also claimed his first two aerial kills), two Silver Stars, four Distinguished Flying Crosses, three Air Medals and four Purple Hearts. Yet it took him over 50 years to get confirmation of his fifth kill to at last make him an ace. All five of House's victories were scored with the Warhawk in 1942-43, the final three being claimed with this machine.

8

P-40E-1 41-25164 of Lt John D Landers, 9th FS, Port Moresby, December 1942

'Whispering John' Landers was a member of Lt Andy Reynolds' esteemed 'Blue Flight'. Having claimed four kills during the defence of Darwin, he 'made ace' on 26 December 1942 when he downed two of six Ki-43s that he intercepted over Dobodura while flying Ben Irvin's P-40E-1 41-25164. Landers had to bail out of the fighter moments later when he was shot up by the remaining 'Oscars'. After completing his combat tour in the Pacific, he went on to achieve greater fame as commander of several Eighth Air Force fighter units. Landers finished the war with a total of 14.5 confirmed aerial and 20 strafing victories.

9

P-40E-1 41-35972 'Yellow 43' of Lt Bill Day, 8th FS, Port Moresby, March 1943

Bill Day served in the 8th FS throughout the unit's defence of Darwin but did not score his first victory until moving to Port Moresby. He opened his account on 1 November 1942 with a Zero, and claimed two more naval fighters (in this machine) on 7 January 1943. Day was again flying *JERRY II* on 11 March when he shot down a Zeke and a G4M 'Betty' off the coast of New Guinea for his fourth and fifth victories, making him the first 8th FS pilot to become an ace in New Guinea proper. He spent some 28 months in the south-west Pacific area before returning to the US in

April 1944. This P-40E, which was the second assigned to Day during his combat tour, carried the name *MARY-WILLIE* on right side of its nose, and had four yellow bomb 'spokes' on each wheel hub.

10

P-40K (serial unknown) 'White 34' of Lt Donald H Lee Jr, 7th FS, Dobodura, spring 1943

Involved in the defence of Darwin, Donald Lee Jr went on to see combat with the unit in New Guinea in 1942-43. By the time he finished his combat tour in the summer of 1943 Lee had downed two Zeros, an 'Oscar' and a 'Val'.

11

P-40K (serial unknown) 'Yellow 15' of Capt George Manning, 7th FS, Four-Mile Strip, December 1942

Manning scored his one and only victory during the defence of Darwin in June 1942, flying a P-40E. Promoted to squadron 'ops exec', he had moved with the 7th FS to New Guinea by year-end, where he flew this P-40K on numerous defensive patrols.

12

P-40E (serial unknown) 'Yellow 49' of Maj Ellis Wright, V Fighter Command HQ, Dobodura, May 1943

Wright earned his wings in 1940 and was stationed in Hawaii at the time of the Pearl Harbor attack. He joined the 49th FG in late 1942 as 8th FS operations executive, often flying this colourful P-40E. He transferred to V Fighter Command as assistant operations director in March 1943, by which time he had three confirmed victories to his credit. On 11 April 1943 Wright shot down three Zeros in a single engagement while defending Allied shipping in Oro Bay, taking his victory total to six. He rotated back to the US in June 1943, but returned to combat during the Korean War.

13

P-38G-13 43-2208 'White 95' of Capt Bill Haney, 9th FS, Dobodura, October 1943

Flight leader Bill Haney had a hard time getting his victories confirmed, although in his own mind, and in the eyes of his squadronmates, he was an ace. His official score stands at two confirmed and five probables. Haney flew this machine, complete with flight leader bands and enlarged identifying numbers, during the Rabaul operations of 29 October and 2 November 1943. He claimed several unconfirmed victories during the course of these missions.

14

P-38H-1 (serial unknown) 'White 79' of Capt Dick Bong, 9th FS, Dobodura, September 1943

Flown by Bong upon his return from the 35th FG in mid 1943, this aircraft had seen much combat by the time it was written off in a landing accident at Marilinan on 6 September. With his tally then standing at 16 kills, Bong ended up putting his fighter in a ditch after he lost power while coming in to land. His machine had been damaged by defensive fire from two 'Bettys' that he had attacked over Morobe. Despite seeing the bombers trailing smoke after his attacks, Bong was only credited with two probables. His Lightning, however, was declared a write-off.

15

P-38G-5 (serial unknown) 'White 73' of Lt Dick Bong, 9th FS, Dobodura, July 1943

Dick Bong reportedly used this machine to claim a Ki-43 destroyed northwest of Rein Bay on 28 July 1943 while escorting 3rd Air Group B-25s that had been sent to bomb shipping off New Britain and an air strip at Cape Gloucester. A large formations of 'Oscars' had sortied from Rabaul in response to the raid, and the ten 9th FS P-38s and twelve P-39s of the 39th FS were hard-pressed to keep the Japanese fighters away from the B-25s. Nevertheless, the American pilots stuck to their job, and no fewer than seven Ki-43s were claimed to have been destroyed by the P-38s. One of these fell to Dick Bong (for his 16th kill), but not before the upper surface of his left wing had been struck five times by 7.7mm machine gun rounds fired by a diving 'Oscar'. Bong's P-38 was the only one to be hit in the sortie, and it was duly taken out of service for repairs to be effected. This was possibly the only time he flew 'White 73', for his assigned mount at this time was 'White 79'. Note the white eye motif adorning the engine intake fairing.

16

P-40K (serial unknown) 'White 16' of Lt Clyde V Knisley, 7th FS, Dobodura, July 1943

Knisley's only score was a Zeke damaged on the 3 July 1943 Mubo mission. He was flying 'White 16' at the time.

17

P-40N (serial unknown) 'Yellow 57' of Capt Richard J Vodra, 8th FS, Marilinan, autumn 1943

Vodra downed two Zekes with this aircraft in the 8th FS's big serial battle over Oro Bay on 14 May 1943. He later decorated the rudder of his P-40N with black checks in the autumn of 1943 at Marilinan. Vodra was responsible for obtaining a Disney cartoon of a 'black sheep' from a friend at the studio which duly became the 8th FS mascot, and gave the squadron its nickname.

18

P-40N (serial unknown) 'White 16' of Capt Nathaniel H Blanton, 7th FS, Dobodura, autumn 1943

Almost an ace, 'Baldy' Blanton scored three kills with the 17th PS over Java in early 1942 and then downed a Zero and probably destroyed another over Darwin on 14 June that same year. He failed to add to his tally in New Guinea.

19

P-38G-13 43-2204 'White 99' of Lt John G O'Neill, 9th FS, Dobodura, autumn 1943

Joining the 49th FG in September 1942, 'Jump' O'Neill scored six of his eight kills (all fighters) between 15 and 29 October 1943 during the height of the Rabaul offensive. He flew this P-38 during the final months of his tour, which ended in November 1943 when he was transferred home.

20

P-38H-1 (serial unknown) 'White 83' of Capt Gerald Johnson, 9th FS, Dobodura, November 1943

P-38H-1 'White 83' was inherited by Jerry Johnson when he replaced future ETO 'ace-in-a-day' Maj Sid Woods as CO of the 9th FS in August 1943. It was marked as aircraft 'White 92' when assigned to Woods, although Johnson soon had this changed to his favoured 'White 83'. Command stripes were also added to the twin tails. He flew this machine on a number of the long range bomber escort missions performed by the 9th FS in support of the Allied bombing campaign against the Japanese stronghold of Rabaul in October-November 1943. These sorties were arduous for both the pilots and their aircraft, and the unit could barely muster 12 serviceable P-38s throughout this period. Nevertheless, 9th FS pilots proved their aerial superiority by downing 22 kills in just four missions – at least three of these fell to Johnson in this very machine.

21

P-40N-5 (serial unknown, possibly 42-105405) 'White 13' of Lt Bob DeHaven, 7th FS, Gusap, January 1944

Bob DeHaven would score ten of his eventual fourteen victories flying P-40s with the 7th FS, making him equal top of the list for USAAF Warhawk aces in the Pacific theatre. He claimed his first victory in a P-40K on 14 July 1943 and his fifth in this aircraft on 10 December. Like many aircraft in the squadron, this machine carried different artwork on either side of its nose, with a white and purple orchid adorning the lower left cowling and the name *Rita* applied in white script on the lower right cowling. DeHaven later flew two other P-40Ns before eventually converting to the P-38 in the autumn of 1944, and he used the Lockheed fighter to increase his score to 14 confirmed victories.

22

P-47D (serial unknown) 'White 80' of Lt James D Haislip, 9th FS, Gusap, January 1944

James Haislip flew P-40s and P-47s (his machine featuring a flight leader's stripe) with the 9th FS, before finally transitioning to P-38s in the spring of 1944. He claimed his solitary victory (a 'Val') in a Lightning on 28 July 1944.

23

P-40N (serial unknown) 'White 24' of Lt Elliott Dent, 7th FS, Gusap, January 1944

Dent scored the first of his three P-40 victories on 3 July 1943, just six weeks after joining the 7th FS. His next chance to score came six months later, on 23 January 1944, when he shot down two Zeros near Cape Torabu in this near new P-40N. He achieved three more victories during a single mission in November 1944 after his squadron had transitioned to P-38s. The red border on the national markings of Dent's P-40N identifies it as a replacement aircraft delivered to the 49th FG in late 1943.

24

P-47D-5 (serial unknown) 'White 83' of Maj Gerald Johnson, 9th FS, Gusap, January 1944

The 9th FS was forced to part with its beloved P-38s following the attritional Rabaul campaign, as Lockheed could not supply enough fighters to make good the heavy losses suffered by the 'Flying Knights'. There was no such shortage of P-47s, and the 9th duly converted onto Republic's heavyweight Thunderbolt in late November 1943. Johnson and his men were less than impressed with the P-47D-4, and the 9th FS was the only unit within the 49th FG to fly the fighter. As if to prove their point, just three of the unit's aces scored kills with the P-47, including

Johnson, who managed to claim a 'Tony' and a Zeke destroyed in December 1943 and January 1944 respectively. The 9th FS claimed a paltry eight victories in total during its five-month association with the Thunderbolt. Johnson primarily flew this particular machine (serial unknown) up until he was posted to command school on 29 January 1944, the P-47 featuring his full tally, his favourite side number '83' and standard white theatre identification markings and command stripes.

25

P-40N (serial unknown) 'White 19' of Capt Duncan Myers, 7th FS, Gusap, January 1944

Myers flew E-, K- and N-model P-40s in combat, and he rated this particular machine as his favourite. He missed out on becoming an ace through the toss of a coin, as the disputed kill was credited to his wingman, Lt Logan Jarman – this happened to Myers on one other occasion also! This form of kill accreditation was unique to the 49th FG, as other fighter units in the USAAF awarded shared kills. Therefore, the unfortunate Myers would have been an ace in any other unit.

26

P-47D (serial unknown) 'White 91' of Capt Wally Jordan, 9th FS, Gusap, March 1944

Wally Jordan was one of just a handful of 9th FS pilots to claim a victory with the P-47, the unit CO downing an 'Oscar' on 14 March 1944. This doubled his score, for he had destroyed a Ki-43 on 2 August 1943 while flying a P-38H-1. Jordan had taken over command of the 9th when Jerry Johnson was sent to command school on 29 January 1944. As with Johnson's Thunderbolt, Jordan had his machine marked with command stripes mid fuselage.

27

P-40N-5 42-105405 'White 28' of Lt Jack A Fenimore, 7th FS, Hollandia, May 1944

The risqué nose art on this aircraft was derived from an old drinking song. Fenimore's only victory came in 'White 28' on 15 May 1944, when he downed an 'Oscar' off Biak Island.

28

P-38L-5 (serial unknown) 'Black 91' of Maj Wally Jordan, 49th FG HQ, Biak, October 1944

By the time Wally Jordan was issued with this aircraft in late October 1944, he had claimed all six of his kills – three of these had come earlier that same month in another P-38L-1. Although a member of the 49th FG HQ flight, he kept his aircraft 'stabled' with his old unit, the 9th FS, hence its red spinners. Also note the fighter's 49th FG staff stripes forward of the twin fins. With the coming invasion of the Philippines, pre-war Army Air Corps tri-colour rudder markings were adopted by several USAAF groups, including the 49th FG.

29

P-38L-5 (serial unknown) 'Black 83' of Maj Gerald Johnson, 49th FG, Biak, October 1944

This particular aircraft was used by Maj Johnson for much of the Philippines campaign in late 1944, the aircraft featuring no personal markings other than his ever-growing scoreboard and his favourite number '83' on the nose and radiator fairings. Johnson claimed ten kills between 14 October and 7 December 1944, and some of these were achieved at the controls of this machine.

30

P-40N-5 42-105826 'Black 7' of Maj Gerald Johnson, 49th FG HQ, Biak, October 1944

Upon Johnson's return to the 49th FG from leave in the late summer of 1944, he had been appointed Group Ops Executive. As a perk of the job, he acquired this P-40N which had recently been retired by the 7th FS – the latter unit had finally converted to Lightnings in September 1944. Johnson had the fighter stripped back to bare metal and its armament and protective armour removed. The end result was a gleaming, high performance hack that he would regularly use to embarrass novice P-38 pilots in mock dogfights over nearby Sentani Lake.

31

P-38L-5 (serial unknown) 'Black 13' of Capt Bob DeHaven, 7th FS, Tacloban, November 1944

7th FS Ops Executive Bob DeHaven was another veteran ace who enjoyed himself in the target rich skies over Leyte in the autumn of 1944. He claimed four kills and one damaged between 29 October and 4 November, and all of these victories were probably achieved in this P-38L-5. Quite possibly one of the ex-8th or 475th FG Lightnings hastily commandeered as attrition replacements by the 49th FG in early November, this aircraft was marked with the appropriate blue squadron colours of the 7th FS. And although the fighter did not feature either DeHaven's name or scoreboard beneath the cockpit, someone had still found the time to adorn its twin fins with the unit's Bunyap emblem synonymous with the 7th FS. DeHaven's P-38L-5 was reportedly destroyed in a bombing raid soon after its pilot returned home on leave in mid November 1944.

32

P-38L-1 44-23964 'Yellow 42' of Maj Dick Bong, V Fighter Command, Tacloban, November 1944

Marked up in 8th FS colours, P-38L-1 44-23964 was Maj Bong's mount during his attachment to the 49th FG as gunnery instructor throughout the Philippines campaign – he had returned to combat in the autumn of 1944 for his third tour, ostensibly in a non-combat role as V Fighter Command's senior gunnery instructor. Sensing the opportunity for more aerial kills with the impending retaking of the Philippines, Bong contacted 49th FG CO Lt Col George Walker and asked him if he could fly attached to his old group for a while. The colonel readily agreed, and commandeered brand new P-38L-1 44-23964 from the 8th FS to serve as Bong's personal mount. The ace would claim six kills with the fighter between 10 October and 11 November 1944, taking his score to 36 victories. 44-23964 was subsequently lost while being flown by 49th FG Deputy Ops Officer Maj John Davis on 28 November, the pilot perishing when the fighter stalled in soon after taking off from Tacloban.

33

P-38J (serial unknown) of Capt Sammy Pierce, 8th FS, Tacloban, December 1944

This remarkably plain Lightning was probably the aircraft

Pierce was flying on 26 December 1944 when he downed three Zeke 52s (with a fourth as a probable) and a 'Tojo' over Clark Field to give him ace status – he had three kills from his days flying a P-40E. Pierce's last kill of the day was shot down in front of Maj Tommy McGuire.

34

P-38L-5 44-25327 'Black 19' of Lt Fernley Damstrom, 7th FS, Tacloban, spring 1945

The 49th FG's leading ace of the Philippines campaign, Damstrom claimed eight kills between 2 November and 20 December 1944. He was killed in a take-off accident in this machine on 11 April 1945.

35

P-38L-5 44-27121 'Black 1' of Maj James A Watkins, 49th FG, Lingayen, spring 1945

Watkins returned to the 49th late in the war, but did not participate in many aerial combats. However, he did manage to shoot down a Ki-44 on 2 April 1945 when he accompanied Lt Col Jerry Johnson to Hong Kong.

36

P-38L-5 44-25638 'Black 10' of Maj Clayton M Isaacson, 9th FS, Lingayen, spring 1945

Isaacson had already claimed five kills in P-38s with the 82nd FG in the Mediterranean by the time he transferred to the 49th FG in February 1945 for what would be his third combat tour. He flew 82 missions with the group, but did not to add to his aerial tally.

37

P-38L (serial unknown) 'Black 73' of Lt James Haislip, 9th FS, Lingayen, spring 1945

Jimmie Haislip flew all three fighter types operated by the 9th FS in World War 2, with this particular P-38L being his final mount in the Pacific.

38

P-38L-5 44-25568 'Silver 44' of Maj George Laven Jr, 49th FG, Lingayen, spring 1945

Laven was a colourful character whose ambition was to become an ace. He accomplished this to his satisfaction on 26 April 1945 when he shot down a Kawanishi H8K 'Emily' flying boat, but the Army Air Force would not confirm his previous four victory claims in Alaska.

39

P-38L-5 (serial unknown) 'Black 10' of Lt Col Clay Tice Jr, 49th FG, Lingayen, August 1945

Tice flew a combat tour with the 9th FS in 1942/43, during which he scored two combat victories. He returned in 1945 to take command of the 49th FG, and on 16 August became the first American to land an aeroplane on mainland Japan when he put this very machine down at Nittagahara airfield when his wingman ran low on fuel.

40

P-38L-5 44-26407 'Black 84' of Maj Jim Watkins, 49th FS, Lingayen, July 1945

This was the second of two P-38L-5s to be assigned to 'Duckbutt' Watkins during his second combat tour with the 49th FG, and like his P-38G-10 from 1943, he marked it up with the name of his sweetheart.

INDEX

References to illustrations are shown in **bold**. Plates are shown with page and caption locators in brackets.